Known & little-k

Volcanoes

of the Massif central

À Mireille, l'inspiratrice.

Éditions DEBAISIEUX

CONTENTS

Introduction 4
The Chaîne des Puys 12
From the Limagne to the Montbrison basin 34
The Monts Dore 42
The Cézalier 58
The Monts du Cantal 64
The Aubrac 82
The Devès and the basin of Le Puy-en-Velay 90
The Emblavès, the Haut-Velay and the Ardèche mountains 100
The Ardèche Cévenne and the Coiron 112
The volcanisme of the Causses, the Escandorgue and the Bas-Languedoc 118
Glossary 126
Maps, cross sections & diagrams

The Coupe d'Aizac and its crater, near Vals-les-Bains in the Ardèche.

"The Auvergne is not accessible to everybody", said Edouard Martel, the father of speleology, a hundred years ago. What this forerunner in the field of earth sciences meant is that the strange features of this region may only be appreciated if we understand the volcanic mechanisms at work.

Another pioneer, Haroun Tazieff said* : « I came to the Auvergne volcanoes after fifteen years travelling the world in search of volcanic eruptions. I now know that if I had first "learnt my lessons" in our Puys, on the slopes of the Cantal and the Mont-Dore, I would have gained precious time... Whereas over there, the excessiveness of the sight defied both reasoning and objectivity, here everything leads to an understanding, to quiet discussion, to the analysis of telluric phenomena. »

But an eruption on the other side of the world may help us to understand certain aspects of the extinct volcanoes of the Massif Central...

*RUDEL Aimé, *Les volcans d'Auvergne*, Éditions Volcans.

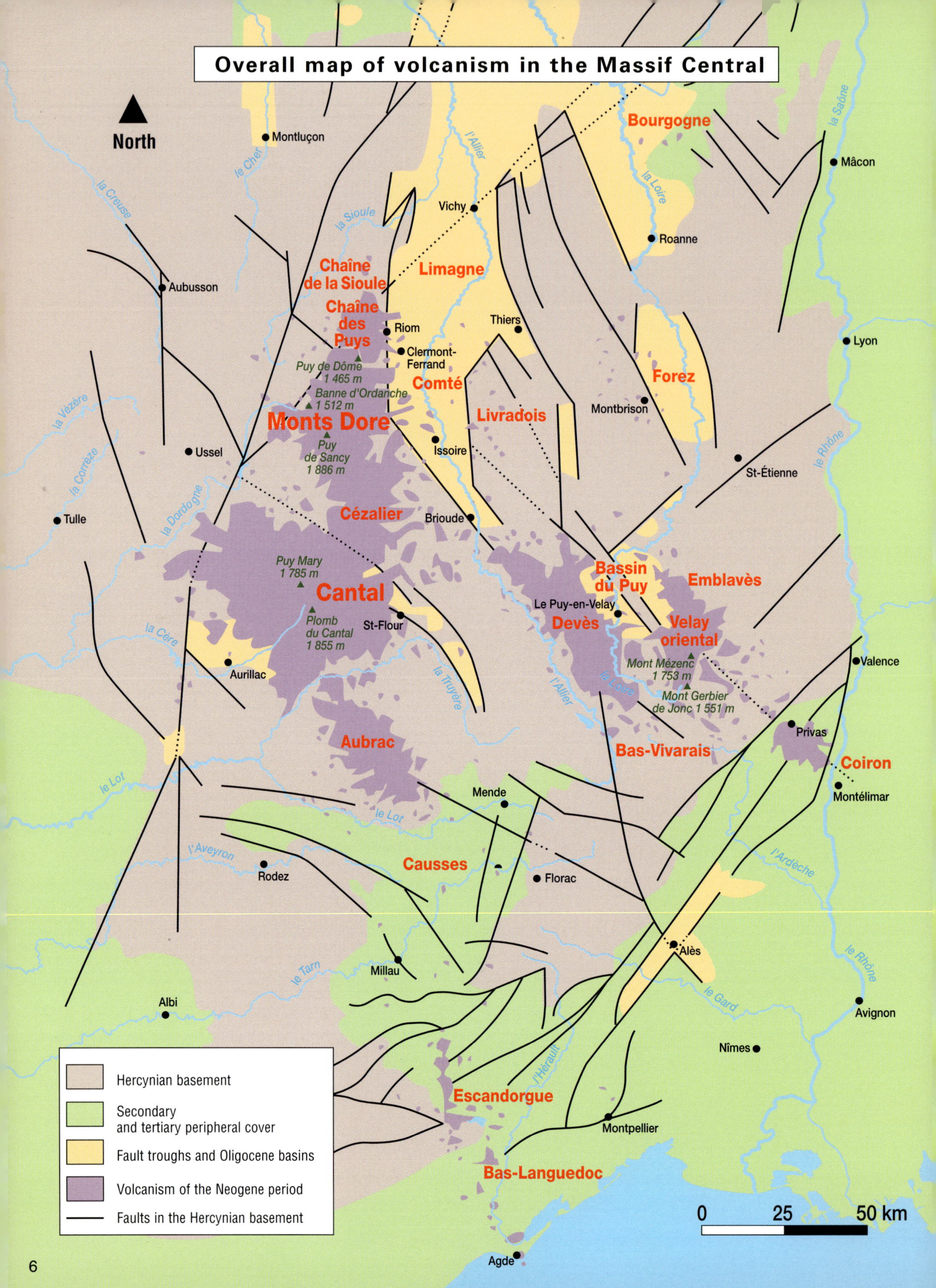

Overall map of volcanism in the Massif Central
North
Montluçon
le Cher
la Creuse
la Sioule
l'Allier
Bourgogne
la Saône
Mâcon
la Loire
Vichy
Roanne
Aubusson
Chaîne de la Sioule
Limagne
Chaîne des Puys
Riom
Thiers
Clermont-Ferrand
Lyon
Puy de Dôme 1 465 m
Banne d'Ordanche 1 512 m
Comté
Forez
la Vézère
Livradois
Montbrison
Monts Dore
Puy de Sancy 1 886 m
Issoire
le Rhône
Ussel
St-Étienne
la Corrèze
la Dordogne
Tulle
Cézalier
Brioude
Puy Mary 1 785 m
Bassin du Puy
Emblavès
Cantal
Plomb du Cantal 1 855 m
St-Flour
Le Puy-en-Velay
Devès
Velay oriental
la Cère
Aurillac
la Truyère
Mont Mézenc 1 753 m
Valence
l'Allier
la Loire
Mont Gerbier de Jonc 1 551 m
Privas
Aubrac
Bas-Vivarais
Coiron
le Lot
Montélimar
Mende
le Lot
l'Aveyron
Rodez
Causses
Florac
l'Ardèche
Alès
le Rhône
le Tarn
Millau
le Gard
Albi
Avignon
Nîmes
l'Hérault
Escandorgue
Montpellier
Bas-Languedoc
Agde
Hercynian basement
Secondary and tertiary peripheral cover
Fault troughs and Oligocene basins
Volcanism of the Neogene period
Faults in the Hercynian basement
0
25
50 km

Mountains from the depths of the earth

For a long time, the volcanoes of the Auvergne were just ordinary mountains; then in 1751 the Parisian naturalist Jean-Etienne Guettard became aware of the special nature of these landforms. Twenty-five years later, the French Academy of Sciences accepted reality and the volcanoes of the Massif Central excited more and more interest. Where do we stand today? To understand why volcanoes occurred in the Auvergne, we have to look back. The eruptive phenomena should be looked at in terms of the globe, the surface of which is made up of continental plates "floating" on the molten rocks of the lower mantle. Therefore, continental drift explains that the Alps are the result of the collision between the Eurasian and African plates.

The formation of this new chain of mountains fractured the old granitic basement which surrounded it and the underlying molten rock was able to rise up. Volcanic activity appeared in the Massif Central, but also in Germany and in Bohemia, along an aborted rift, known as the Rhone-Rhine rift.

Above - *The crests of the Cantal seen from Puy Mary, with Puy Griou in the distance and the Plomb du Cantal on the horizon.*
Below - *In the Chaîne des Puys, the perfect crater of the Pariou.*

The rise of magma sets up complex phenomena which are still not fully understood. Magma is a pasty material produced by the fusion of part of the outer layers of the earth, the surface crust and the upper part of the mantle, on which it lies. In the Massif Central, this occurred at a depth of between 100 and 150 km. Like a hot air balloon, the resulting hot pocket, known as a diapir, works its way upwards and may reach the surface directly, retaining its original composition. In this case, the eruption will be basaltic.
But if this pocket is slowed down, its composition changes due to the crystallisation of part of its elements and the proportion of dissolved gases will increase. In the Massif Central, where volcanism is of the continental type, unlike basalt, which is fluid and basic, we find rhyolite, a very viscous and acidic rock. Its chemical composition is the same as that of granite: granite is formed by magma which did not reach the surface and crystallised slowly at depth. Of course, all intermediate variations exist, with the great groups of lavas: trachybasalts, basaltic trachyandesites, trachy-andesites and trachytes.
Furthermore, many volcanic rocks are modified, being loose or cemented accumulations of various fragments. Such debris comes from fresh magmas, lavas that have already cooled or even underlying rocks, whether crystalline or sedimentary... Such rocks known as pyroclastics, are produced by gaseous explosions, but also by avalanches of debris and mud slides which accompany major eruptions.

Fireworks of all kinds

Recent research leads us to think that the Massif Central has two levels of magma chamber with a large pocket at the boundary between the mantle and the crust, at a depth of twenty five to thirty kilometres and a series of small independent chambers, at between five and fifteen kilometres.

Above - *The Rocher de Laqueuille a neck in the Santoire valley (Cantal).*
Inset - *The Roche Sanadoire, in the Monts Dore, with the Puy de Dôme in the distance; the Veyrines falls, near Allanche (Cantal).*

Volcanism in the Auvergne began in Burgundy, in the Charolais, 65 million years ago, at the beginning of the Tertiary period. These eruptions were limited, but spread over a period of 25 million years, and also later concerned the Menat region, where a maar became famous for the fossils from the sediments of its former lake. These two periods of volcanic activity lasted a long time, but we should also note that the first eruptions occurred at this time in the Causses, the Forez and Bas Languedoc, where activity continued throughout the Tertiary period, if not longer.

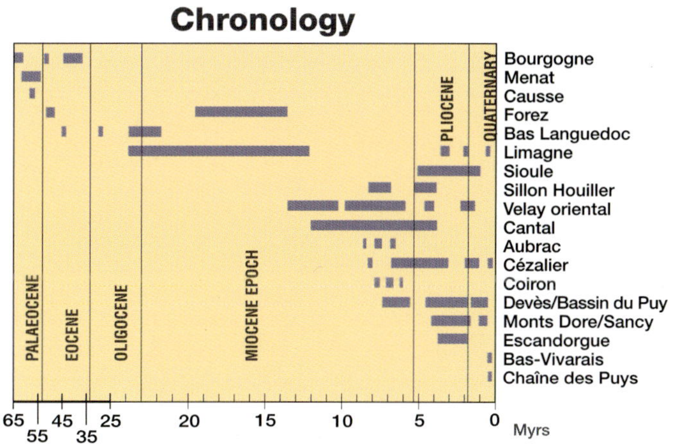

The chateau of Busséol, on a volcanic neck.

Is it possible for a dormant volcano to erupt?

The eastern Velay, the Cantal, Aubrac, Cézalier, Coiron and Devès began to form about 10 million years ago. Then came the Monts Dore and the Escandorgue and, very recently in geological terms, the volcanoes of the Cévenne in the Ardèche and the Chaîne des Puys appeared.
The fact that later eruptions occurred on the edge of the Massif Central lead us to think that the main magma chamber was blocked and that the exit points moved further along the main fractures. Given what preceded, one is tempted to assume that eruptions may begin again on the margins of the massif since the present silence of the volcanoes in this region is only dormancy. During the very brief Quaternary period, volcanic activity occurred in dozens of areas.
Geologists cannot tell the location of the next eruption, but in no case will it be one of the volcanoes making up the Chaîne des Puys, as fear some Auvergnats.

Left - *The neck of the Rocher d'Aiguilhe, on which a 10th century chapel is built.*
Right - *The Déroc falls, at the front of a basalt flow in the Aubrac.*

Statistically, the most probable is a basaltic eruption, which is highly spectacular but relatively calm, of the type of the Puy volcanoes.
Other far rarer eruptions are more dangerous, such as those that occur at the same time as protrusions, with their nuées ardentes. Furthermore, if rising magma meets a body of water underground or on the surface, the resulting "phreatomagmatic" eruption becomes highly explosive and destructive. Nor can they predict the date of such a resumption in volcanic activity, but they will not be taken by surprise, since cataclysmic eruptions never occur without precursory signs. The rise of magma is accompanied by minor earthquakes which would be recorded by the many seismographs installed in the Massif Central.

Above - *Near Lake of Guéry, the Roches Tuilière and Sanadoire, necks exposed by glaciers during the Quaternary period.*
Below - *At Arlempdes, the upper Loire winds its way between volcanic cliffs.*

The volcanoes of the Chaîne des Puys around the Puy de Dôme.

The Chaîne des Puys

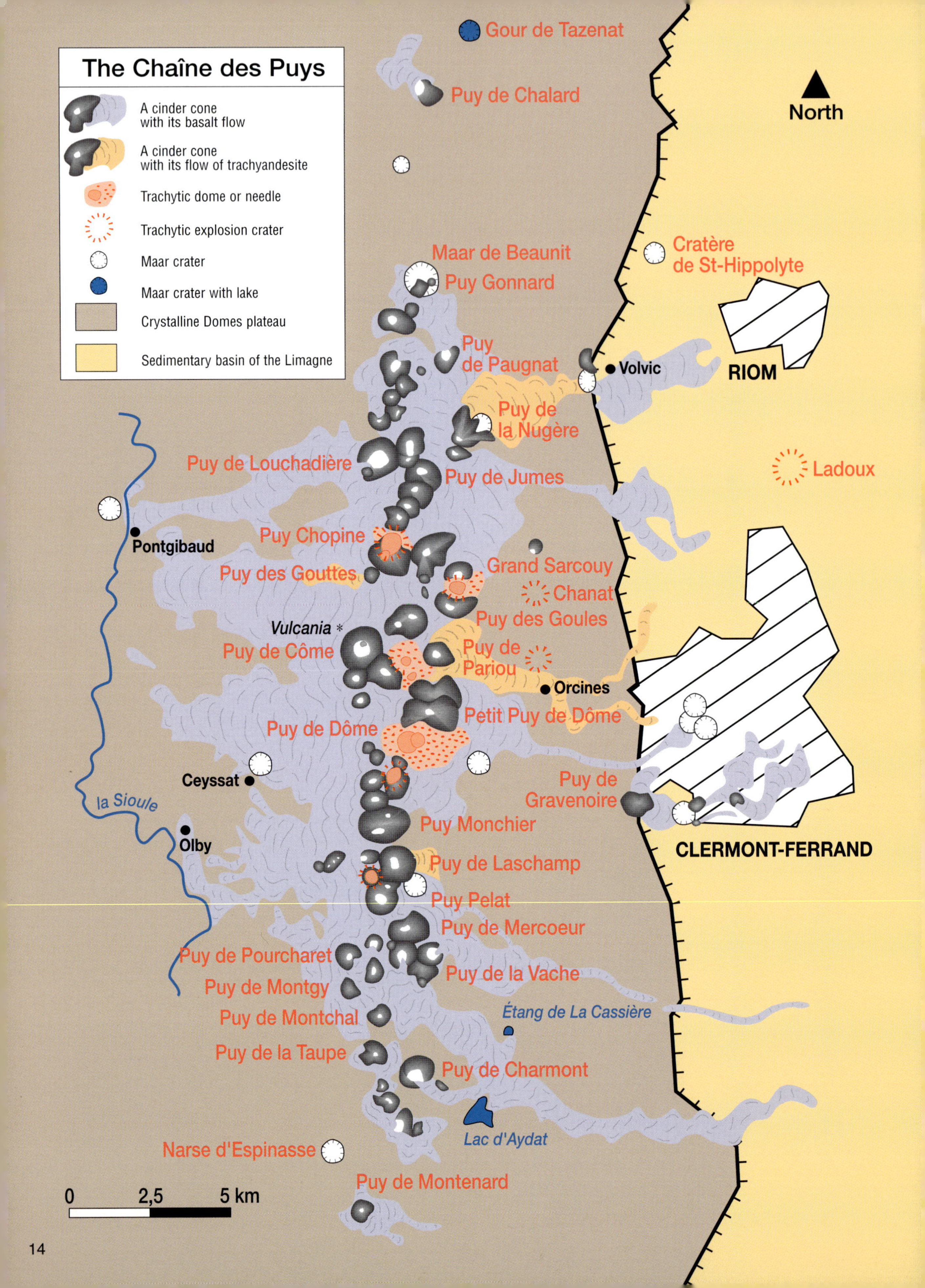
The Chaîne des Puys
A cinder cone with its basalt flow
A cinder cone with its flow of trachyandesite
Trachytic dome or needle
Trachytic explosion crater
Maar crater
Maar crater with lake
Crystalline Domes plateau
Sedimentary basin of the Limagne
North
Gour de Tazenat
Puy de Chalard
Maar de Beaunit
Puy Gonnard
Cratère de St-Hippolyte
RIOM
Puy de Paugnat
Volvic
Puy de la Nugère
Ladoux
Puy de Louchadière
Puy de Jumes
Pontgibaud
Puy Chopine
Puy des Gouttes
Grand Sarcouy
Chanat
Puy des Goules
Vulcania
Puy de Côme
Puy de Pariou
Orcines
Petit Puy de Dôme
Puy de Dôme
Ceyssat
la Sioule
Puy de Gravenoire
Puy Monchier
Olby
CLERMONT-FERRAND
Puy de Laschamp
Puy Pelat
Puy de Mercoeur
Puy de Pourcharet
Puy de la Vache
Puy de Montgy
Étang de La Cassière
Puy de Montchal
Puy de la Taupe
Puy de Charmont
Lac d'Aydat
Narse d'Espinasse
Puy de Montenard
0
2,5
5 km

With their craters and domes aligned for some forty kilometres like a procession overlooking Clermont-Ferrand, the Puys are the standard bearers of volcanism in the Massif Central. Looking at their intact forms around the giant guardian of the Puy de Dôme (1,465 m) it is easy to imagine the inferno at their peaks. Despite their general youth, these volcanoes took more than 70,000 years to form their line. Furthermore, without exception, all of them were produced by a single eruption of a few days or months; the Puy de Dôme itself, the longest to be formed, probably appeared in less than two years. The Chaîne has therefore been dormant, as now, for most of its existence.

In the northern part of the Chaîne des Puys, the craters of the Puys des Goules and the Pariou.

Dispersed eruptions as a prelude

These famous volcanoes did not appear "suddenly". After the Monts Dore massif fell dormant, 250,000 years ago, volcanic activity never completely died out in the region. Modern dating methods have revealed that eruptions occurred in the north of the Cézalier, to the north of the Monts Dore, near the Sioule, on the edge of the Limagne with the maars of Jaude (150,000 years) and Saint-Hippolyte (93,000 years), on the plateau des Dômes with the Puy de Chanat (90,000 years) and to the south of Clermont, the Puy de Boisséjour on the plateau Saint-Jacques (82,000 years). To the north, the maar of Menat was formed 60 million years ago. The Limagne plain was the scene of eruptions 24 to 12 million years ago, and the Olby basin saw several basalt flows. The Gergovia plateau, the Côtes de Clermont and the plateau of Chateaugay are 16 million years old. The Charade and Montagne Percée flows date back 3 million years and were formed before those of Berzet and Saint-Genès-Champanelle.

Below top - *The line of volcanoes of the Chaîne des Puys and the basaltic plateau of the Côtes de Clermont.*
Below bottom - *The Gergovia plateau, one of the fine examples of inverted relief on the edges of the Limagne.*

Above - *The Chaîne des Puys seen from the west, with the Puy de Banson in the Chaîne de la Sioule in the foreground.*
Inset - *The maar of Lake of Anchald, near Pontgibaud.*

The volcanic activity of the Dômes also started in the west with related formations, the small "Chaîne de la Sioule", which remains between Pontgibaud and Manzat in the form of a string of seven relics of basanite flows between 5.4 to 2.1 million years old.
Secondly, we should mention the much more recent Petite Chaîne des Puys, which is an alignment of basalt structure of some importance to the west of the Sioule. The puys de Pranal, Neuffont, Vialle and Banson run from north to south. The road which runs alongside the Sioule and its tributary the Miouze, between Pontgibaud and Rochefort-Montagne is lined with columns of basalt from the Puy de Banson. Opposite, we can see the basalt buttes of Saint-Pierre-le-Chastel and Bonnabaud formed by flows from the Monts Dore.

Above - *The valley of the Sioule up-river of Pontgibaud, an alluvial plain created by a barrier lake formed by flows from the Puy de Côme. In the foreground, Saint-Pierre-le-Chastel, on a flow from the Monts Dore.*

Above - *The crater of the Puy de Pourcharet.*
Below - *Ice which forms in the cavities of cheires (local name for lava flows), even in August.*

The « ice holes » of the cheires de Côme

One of the most surprising results of volcanic activity in the Auvergne takes the form of mysterious ice holes which can be seen at several points in the lava flows of the Puy de Côme and Puys de la Vache and Lassolas. These lava flows are punctuated by depressions of about ten metres in depth. From the bottom of some of them, for example the creux (pits) de Violaine or de l'Aumône, flows cold air, thus forming blocks of ice. This ice used to be used by the local people to treat the sick and one of the holes was used as a ripening cellar for the local blue cheese. The cheires d'Aydat were used for the same purpose for Saint-Nectaire cheese.
Geologists have tried to explain this curiosity. It has been said that this intense cold is due to the evaporation of rain water rising to the surface by capillary action. More recent studies talk of a "seasonal shift" where the porous ground of the lava flows stores winter cold to return it during the summer; but a truly rational explanation for this phenomenon has yet to be provided.

Eighty brand new volcanoes on a very old base

At the very beginning of volcanic activity in the Auvergne, 60 million years ago, the Hercynian chain of the Palaeozoic era, almost completely worn down, was broken up as a result of movements of the earth's crust which affected the Alps and the Mediterranean. In this area, north-south faults caused the collapse of the Limagne plain over a distance of three thousand metres and, to a lesser extent, the Olby basin.

These basins were filled by sediment, then about 20 million years ago, further tectonic movements raised up the crystalline basement throughout the Massif Central. What was to become the plateau des Dômes, a mass of schist, granites and gneiss, was raised up and the margins of this horst were cut into steps by secondary faults.

Below - *The craters of the Puys de Jumes and de la Coquille.*
Inset - *A core of granite from a deep bore in the Chaîne des Puys.*

Above - *The nested craters of the Puy de Côme, the result of two successive eruptions.*
Top left - *A view of the same.* Right - *The breached crater of the Puy de Louchadière.*

Below - *The "grotte des Laveuses" at Royat, showing how water flows under the basalt.*

The Puys of Gravenoire, near Royat, and Bannière, above Volvic, are the only two volcanoes to have erupted on the main Limagne fault. All other eruptions occurred behind, higher up on the plateau and on the same, generally north-south line. Since they are not under compression like the edges of the plateau, secondary faults favoured the rise of magma from a superficial chamber.

The pre-volcanic topography also played its part: the slight westward slope of the horst favoured the spread of wide sheets of lava, for example the "cheires" of the Puys de Côme and Louchadière. To the east, the steeper downslope to the Limagne meant that flows followed the narrow valleys before spreading out at the approaches to the plain. Hence, the basalts of the Petit Puy de Dôme cascaded down the Royat valley before spreading over what is now Chamalières.

After the early basalt days, the magmas became more acidic producing trachyandesites and trachytes; with as their respective main features the Puy de la Nugère, the origin of the flows from which Volvic stone is extracted, and the Puy de Dôme produced by the extrusion of highly viscous lava. Nevertheless, trachyandesites and basalts continued to occur in the Chaîne until eruptions ceased, for example with the Puy du Pariou and the Puys de la Vache and Lassolas respectively.

The cinder cones

Cinder cones, the shape of which symbolise volcanism, are formed by basic magmas, the silica content of which is between approximately 43 and 55% and which contain a high proportion of dissolved gases. It is this gas, which reacts like bubbles in a bottle of champagne, which drives the magma to the surface. It then ejects lava in the form of basalt or trachyandesite. If the gas is abundant, lava, in the form of bombs and ash, builds up to form a cone around the mouth, or, if there is little gas escapes as flows. More often than not, both processes occur at the same time. Such volcanoes are often referred to as Strombolian.

Above left - *The Puy de la Nugère and a quarry of Volvic stone.*
Right - *The extraction of the trachyandesite at Volvic.*
Below left - *The combined craters of the Puy de Barme.*
Right - The former pozzolana quarry in the Puy de Gravenoire.

The breached craters of the Puy de la Vache, on the left, *the Puy de Lassolas,* at the top, *and the Puy de Mey,* on the right.
Inset - *On the lip of the crater of the Puy de la Vache, volcanic blocks emerging out of the pozzolana.*

This type of edifice, which is the most common on earth, is also the best represented in the Chaîne des Puys. Most cinder cones are between one hundred and two hundred metres high. The most imposing, the Puy de Côme (1,253 m) rises to a height of three hundred and fifty metres.
The craters of such volcanoes may take various forms, starting with a simple, regular, completely enclosed depression. The model for this type is the Puy des Goules. Other craters are said to be breached, since they are horse-shoe shaped and open on the side where their lava flows carried off the scoria. The twin Puys de la Vache and Lassolas are the most famous examples of this type.
Several craters may be combined in pairs, such as the Puy de Barme, or in a group of three or four mouths, as in the Puy de Montchier. Much rarer are nested craters, like those of the Puy de Côme, which are the sign of two distinct eruptive phases, from the same mouth. The most famous of these crater volcanoes, the Puy de Pariou (1,209 m), is a special case, since it was formed inside an old explosion crater.
These cones are formed of ejecta of, in ascending order, ash, lapilli or blocks. The pozzolana quarry which has defaced the Puy de Gravenoire, has nevertheless improved our knowledge of volcanism.

Below left - The Puy de Pariou. Right - *The Puy des Goules, another cone with a central crater.*

In this sense, visiting the open air volcano which the Puy de Lemptégy has become is very instructive. It reveals the reddish ejecta of the first volcano, dating back 60,000 years, which were hidden under the black ash of a volcano which erupted 30,400 years ago. In addition, we can see that 8,300 years ago, the nearby Puy Chopine deposited further ejecta and burnt wood on its slopes, together with some of the finest volcanic bombs found on the site.

Above - *The Puy des Gouttes and the Puy Chopine, the last Pelean eruption in the Chaîne, which form a complex edifice.*
Inset - *Scoria mixed with volcanic bombs in the Puy de Lemptégy.*

Cross section of the Puy de Lemptégy

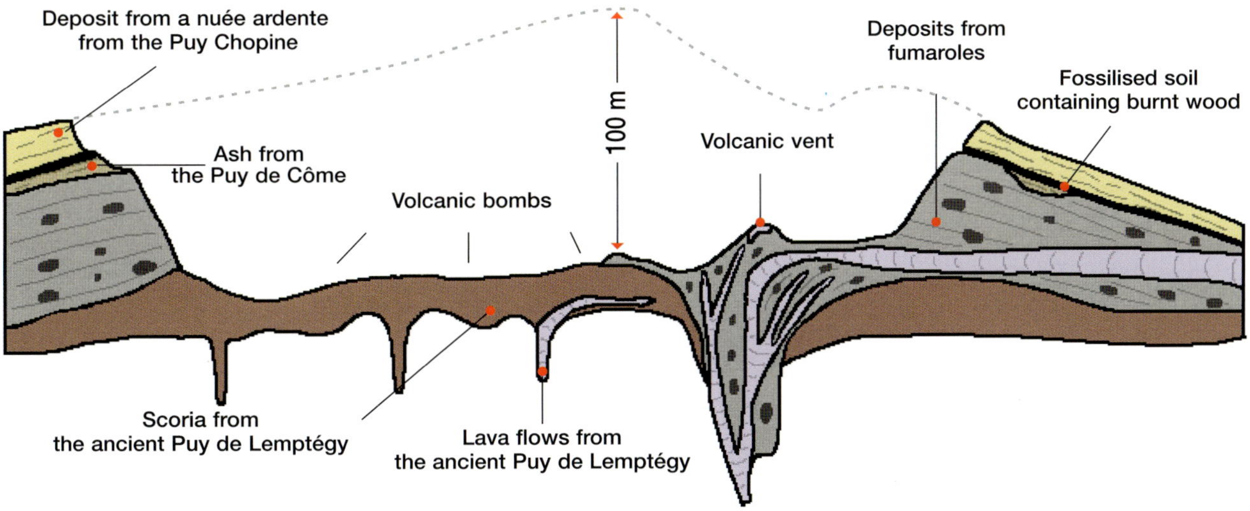

Lava flows and rivers of basalt

The lava flows of the Chaîne des Puys, which appeared in fissures at the base of cinder cones, differ from those of comparable massifs in their relative thinness. They did not cover the entire basement and are only generally twenty metres thick. In exceptional cases, their superimposition can produce some impressive figures, such as the hundred and thirty five metres measured under the "cheires de Côme", for seven superimposed flows. The length of such lava flows may be considerable when they flow down valleys; for example, the basalt flows from the Puys de la Vache and Lassolas which bypassed Saint-Amand-Tallende. In passing, by blocking the valley of the Veyre and one of its tributaries, the flows from these volcanoes formed Lakes of Aydat and La Cassière.

The Puy de Côme and its abundant wooded lava flows with the Puy de Dôme in the distance.
Below - *Tree ferns in Vulcania's volcanic garden.*

Vulcania, the European Park of Volcanism

On the edge of the Chaîne des Puys, Vulcania will provide an outing which is more a voyage of discovery than a museum visit. Outside, Vulcania takes the form of a cone with golden sides. The rest of the architecture is underground, inviting the visitor to descend, first along a gigantic wall covered in volcanic bombs and then into a crater where fumaroles and rumbling noises complete the illusion. Attractively presented, the introduction to volcanism is nevertheless educational and involves geological reconstructions, such as basalt columns, displays on a global scale or a luxuriant garden, which symbolises the fertility of volcanic regions after eruptions.

Highlighted by vegetation, the lava flows from the Puys de la Vache and Lassolas which blocked streams to form Lake of Aydat.

Above - *The twin craters of the Puys de la Vache et de Lassolas and the Puy de Mercœur.*

Below - *Lake of La Cassière with, on the right, rocks from the flow which blocked the valley.*

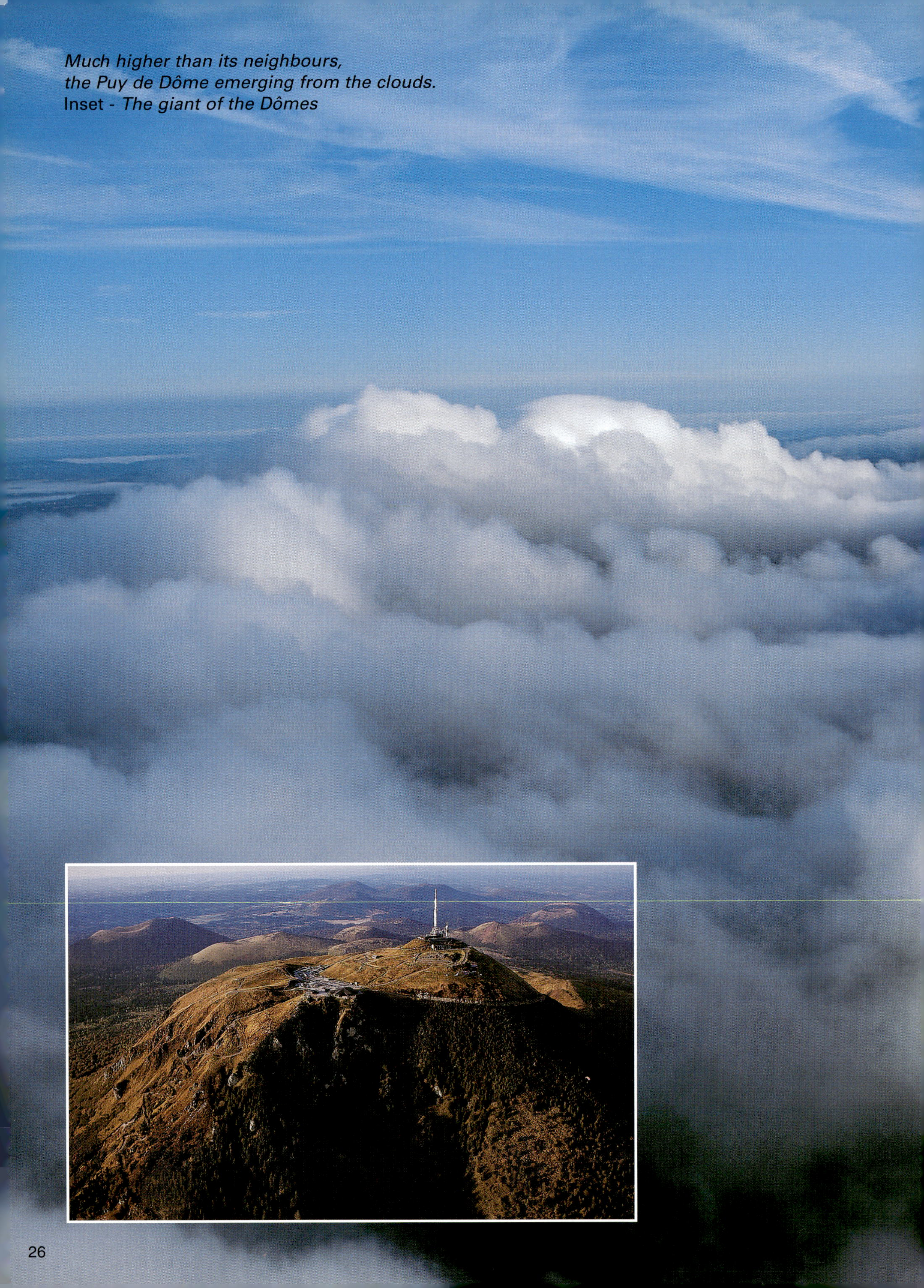

Much higher than its neighbours,
the Puy de Dôme emerging from the clouds.
Inset - *The giant of the Dômes*

Domes and protrusions

Far less common, trachytic volcanoes are formed by viscous lava which accumulates above the vent, in general after an initial explosion. This pasty material collapses sideways, driven up from within by new supplies of magma. Such, so-called Pelean eruptions, are punctuated by nuées ardentes or flows of debris from a partial collapse. If the underlying layer is inclined or presents an obstacle, the dome may become unsymmetrical, as may be seen with the Grand Sarcouy, or Chaudron, between the Puy des Goules and the Petit Sarcouy. Two neighbouring trachytic volcanoes, the Clierzou and the Puy de l'Aumone, or Petit Suchet, have radial crests which are signs of the filling of expansion fissures in their domes.

Above - *The Chaudron, a classic example of trachyte domes.*
Below - *The Petit Suchet and the Clierzou, riddled with caves which are a sign of their trachytic nature.* Inset - *The Clierzou.*

The stepped summit of the Puy de Dôme, which shows the compound nature of the volcano.
Inset - *The only gaseous thermo-mineral spring of the Chaîne, at Ceyssat.*

The term dome leads us to the giant Puy which rises at least two hundred metres above the highest volcanoes in the Chaîne. The Puy de Dôme, a Pelean giant which few other volcanoes of this type in the world can equal, has an irregular shape, which means that its genesis was complex.
About 9,800 years ago, the first trachytic cumulo-dome was formed over an existing Strombolian volcano. Then the entire eastern part of this edifice was destroyed by an explosion which deposited a mass of breccia and ash clouds. A second dome developed in this gash and was briefly capped by a needle comparable to that which rose on Mount Pelée for a few months in 1902-1903. Finally, 8,300 years ago, a huge nuée ardente from the explosion of the Kilian crater, on the col de Ceyssat, covered the entire edifice.

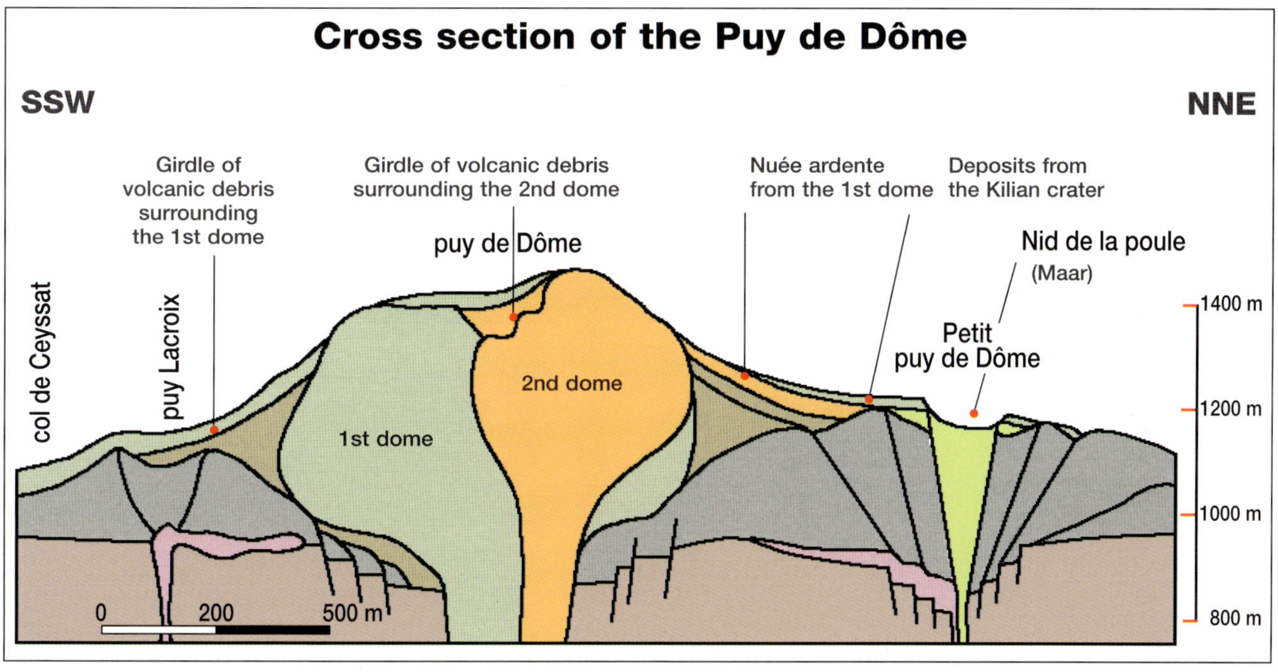

The Kilian crater, together with the Puys Vasset and Chopine, are peculiar examples of trachytic eruptions, since their lava, which is even more viscous than that of the domes, came to the surface virtually solid. So much so, that as it rose the protrusion of the Puy Chopine tore away great blocks of granite from the basement. Protrusions of this type appear after an initial, terribly devastating explosion, accompanied by nuées ardentes. Such violence may be measured by what was torn away from the Puy des Gouttes, in the centre of which the Puy Chopine was formed.

To the north of the Puy de Pariou, debris from a maar has formed a long, rounded crest.

Maars and pyroclastic rings

Maars are the last of the simple volcanic features that may be seen in the Chaîne des Dômes. Their only relief which is not dished is a pyroclastic ring, a mass of explosion debris, like the crescent around the base of the puy de Pariou.
Maars are the results of basaltic and occasionally trachytic "phreatomagmatic" eruptions; the only example of the latter type in the region is that which produced Lake Pavin. The most characteristic maar in the Chaîne is the Gour de Tazenat, isolated to the north of the volcanoes. This, almost perfectly circular lake, fills a crater of almost 700 metres in diameter and 66 metres deep. The unsymmetrical pyroclastic ring is very marked in the north-east part of the crater. The explosion of a maar is always followed by a cloud of basaltic materials which travels horizontally in all directions.

The Gour de Tazenat, shows how an eruption explosive of the maar type removes the ground like a pastry cutter.

A peat bog and a plain succeeded the original lake, with frequent resumption in volcanic activity in the form of a Strombolian edifice. From north to south, the Chaîne shows the maar of Beaunit, which was also partially engulfed by lava flows from the Puy Thiollet, the maar de Volvic, together with the Puy de la Bannière, and those from Chanat, Montchâtre and Villars.

Two remarkable maars lie to the south, the Narses d'Ampoix and d'Espinasse. The first of these peat bogs, which occupies a crater formed 10,700 years ago, has enabled most later eruptions to be dated, since they deposited a bed of ash which was then fossilised by the peat.

Above - *Volvic, a town of water and stone lies on the Limagne fault, with its back to the Puy de la Bannière, the southern part of which was carried off by a maar.*
Left - *Volvic water under the lava flow from the Puy de la Nugère.*

Using this dating method, applied to the "étang de Fung", we think that the last eruption of the Chaîne occurred about 4,000 years ago, but we do not know which Puy. As for the Narse d'Espinasse, it is unusual because the Puy de l'Enfer, the Strombolian edifice adjoining it was formed at the same time as the maar.

Above - *The maar of the Narse d'Espinasse and the small Puy de l'Enfer.*
Below - *The maar of Beaunit, engulfed by a flow highlighted by vegetation.*

In the valley of the Allier, Nonette and its volcanic butte.

From the Limagne to the Montbrison basin

Whilst the Grande Limagne is a perfect sedimentary trough, its southern part, from Riom to Brioude, is studded with innumerable volcanic features. To these buttes may be added lava flows from the Dômes, the Monts Dore and the Cézalier on the western edge of the basin.

Dislodged or inverted by erosion, due to their great age (most of these eruptions date back to the Miocene epoch), these landforms are made up of basalts or basanites. A few volcanoes in the Comté d'Auvergne, cousins of the sucs of the Velay, stand out. These atypical volcanoes, made up of trachyphonolites, appear in the form of domes, such as the Puys de Lachaux-Montgros, and Chaugne and the pic de Vindoux, flow domes, such as the Puys de Sallèdes and Lignol, or even protrusions, like the Puy de Mercurol.

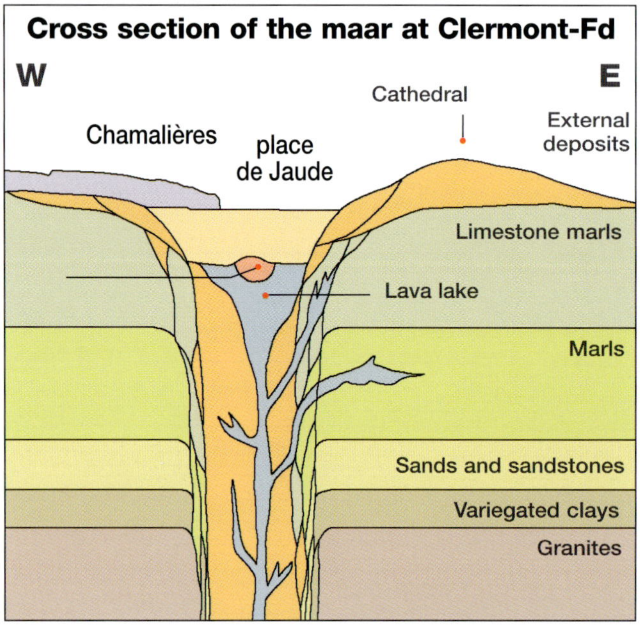

Clermont-Ferrand, with the Puy de Montaudoux in the foreground.

In the land of peperite

The purely Limagne volcanoes are ancient diatremes of a specific pyroclastic rock known as peperite. This is a tuff, produced by basalt mixing with the marls enveloping it. This combination produces a grey to rusty coloured rock with globular granules of lava which look like pepper corns, hence the name.
The "peperite" volcanism of the Limagne began 25 million years ago, when the region was still partially marshy, which explains why the edifices around Cournon, Dallet and Pont-du-Chateau are partially covered in calcareous marl sediments laid down after the eruptions. Volcanic activity occurred in particular between 20 and 12 million years ago, when the plain had dried out and continued sporadically, as shown by one of the most recent volcanoes of this type at Clermont, which is only 150,000 years old. It is the only one which still has its superstructure, which is the butte on which the Cathedral stands.

Above left - *The Piton de Vodable, near Issoire.* Right - *The Puy d'Usson, on the right bank of the Allier.*
Below - *The wine growing village of Corent, nestling against a complex edifice of peperites, pozzolana and basalts.*

Varying forms

Later, basalt lakes filled the craters of these diatremes, above the peperites. The outcrops at Montaudoux and Montrognon, therefore represent a resumption in activity which resulted in the tops of their diatremes being consolidated by basalt. In the absence of such outflows, the depression created by the initial explosive phase was occupied by a lake and filled by sedimentation and may finally have been engulfed by lava flows from neighbouring volcanoes. Occasionally, several scenarios were combined, as in the case of the highly complex Gergovia plateau.

The Puy de Chanturgue, Côtes de Clermont, and, further off, the Côtes de Châteaugay, Puy de Mur and the Montagne de la Serre, the other plateaux surrounding the capital of the Auvergne are the result of the inversion of basalt lava flows.

Below - *The neck at Montrognon near Clermont-Ferrand.* Inset - *The Gros Turluron, near Billom.*
Bottom - *Near Saint-Germain-Lembron, one of the local serres (ridges), an ancient lava flow in the bottom of a valley, exposed by erosion.*

Of the volcanoes formed by purely peperitic eruptions, the Puy de Crouel, on the outskirts of Clermont-Ferrand, clearly shows the hollow stack-of-plates structure specific to the tuffs of diatremes in the Limagne. Another remarkable volcano, the Puy de Corent combines a peperitic diatreme, cinder cone and basalt flow.
The Limagne buttes, the Couzes region, the Comté d'Auvergne and the Livradois, are scattered with dozens of dikes, plugs and necks exposed by erosion. Often spectacular, as at Nonette, where the crag is formed of a special basalt, mandchourite, these landforms have a characteristic shape, such as the Puy d'Ysson or the Grand Turluron, are dark in colour, such as the Roche-Noire, or form superb basalt cliffs, as at Busséol and Buron.

Above - *The butte de Buron, with the ruins of a feudal castle.*
Below - *The stack-of-plates strata of the Puy de Crouel, that are characteristic of peperitic eruptions.*
Inset - *A close up of peperite.*

The dispersed volcanism of the Forez and the Montbrison basin

The Forez is made up of two volcanic edifices about 20 million years old. One is in its mountainous part and the other in the Montbrison basin. On the eastern edge of the crystalline horst, to the east of its highest point Pierre sur Haute (1,634m), the most visible features are the inverted flow at Sauvain and the Mont Semiol, the fragment of a Strombolian volcano covered in sheets of lava. On the crest line, the Grande Pierre Basanne and the Roche Gourgon, in particular, are also of volcanic origin. More spectacular is the Montpeloux butte, between Saint-Anthème and Usson-en-Forez. This neck of basalt is also known as Mont Poilu because of the superb prisms at its base. They rise almost sixty metres above a crater filled with water, an astonishing spectacle revealed by a former quarry.

Above - *The Monts du Forez with the isolated volcanic edifice peak of Chaudabrit in the foreground.*
Left - *Superb basalt columns at Montpeloux.*

At the foot of the highlands, to the west of the Loire, in the sedimentary Montbrison basin, erosion has removed virtually all signs of the volcanism of this period, with the exception of a few outcrops, such as those at Saint-Romain-le-Puy and Montverdun. Some, scarcely visible peperitic edifices, such as that at Fontival, should also be mentioned. A major exception, is the dike of the Mont d'Uzore, which dominates the plain. Extending over a distance of five kilometres, its southern part reveals a wall of lava, some ten to twenty metres high, which becomes an imposing mass of basalt to the north.

Above - *The Puy Saint-Romain, near Montbrison.*
Below top - *The Montverdun butte.*
Bottom - *In the Montbrison basin, the Mont d'Uzore.*

The peaks of the Monts Dore, with the valleys of Chaudefour on the left *and of Le Mont-Dore* on the right, *both characteristic of glacial erosion.*

The Monts Dore

The Chaudefour valley and the pyramidal peak of the Puy de Sancy.
Inset - *The highest point of the Massif Central, in winter.*

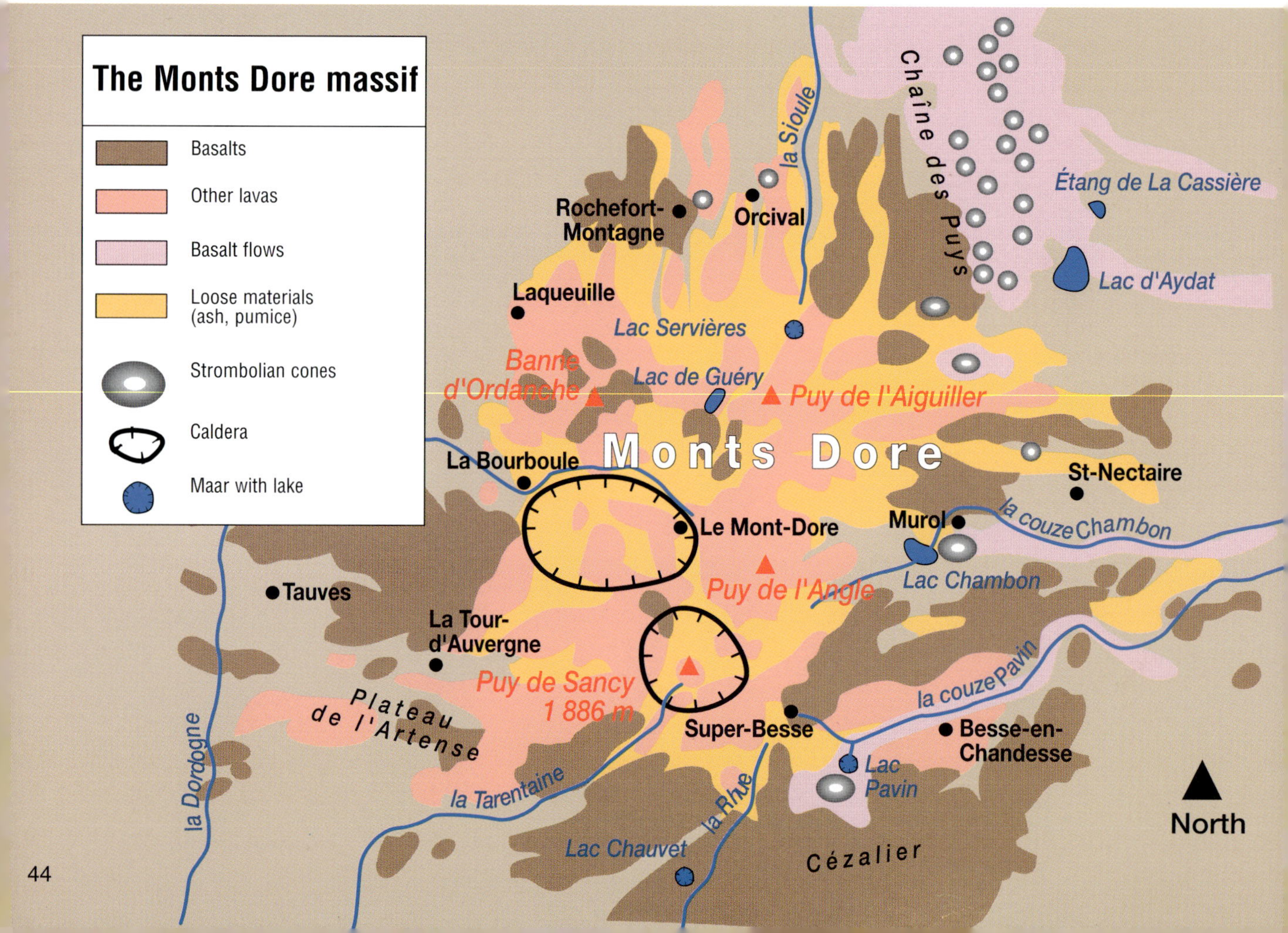

The Monts Dore massif takes the form of a vast low cone, whether seen from the north, from the top of the Puy de Dôme, for example, or from the south, from around Marcenat. The central part of the edifice has no crater, but shows on the contrary, various topographical features, the highest point of which is the Puy de Sancy (1,886 m).

On the map, the Monts Dore describe an elliptical shape and cover almost 600 km^2, three times more than Vesuvius, whilst certain lava flows extend as far as the Limagne. In this case, we should talk of a stratovolcano rather than a volcano, because of the complexity of this massif shaped over an eventful history of almost 4 million years, from the end of the Tertiary period to a relatively recent epoch. Since the appearance of one or more major collapses is typical of stratovolcanoes, we can trace their history in relation to these giant craters known as calderas.

Below - *The Monts Dore seen from the east, with Lake Chambon and the cliffs of the Dent du Marais.*

The crests and needles of the Sancy seen from the south, with the ends of two dikes in the foreground.

Tropical fauna and prehistoric man

When the activity of the Monts Dore began, 3 or 4 million years ago, the climate was much warmer than it is now. Therefore, the fauna which perished under the fires of the Grande Nappe included rhinoceros, tapirs, hyena, sabre toothed tigers, mastodons and ancestors of the elephant and horse. Man did not witness the first great eruption of the Monts Dore, but did see the construction of the massif from afar and was, no doubt victim to it. At Perrier, near Issoire, stones and flints appear to have been shaped by man and fossilised by lahars 2.5 million years ago. Tools of such great age have only been found in east Africa.

Pre-caldera volcanism

The underlying layer of the Monts Dore is formed by the granitic and metamorphic basement of the Palaeozoic era. After first being levelled by erosion, this basement was then subjected to the effects of Alpine folding, which led to the formation of several small fault troughs, soon filled by sediments. Pre-montdorian volcanism appeared on these bases about twenty million years ago, in the form of minor occurrences of basalt. The results of this activity, for example, the plug at Murol, which were covered by material from the strato-volcano, are still visible today. Between 5 and 3 million years ago other, more abundant, basanitic lava flows, were degraded into red clay by the tropical climate of the time. To the north, lies the planeze of Aurières, which extends as far as the northern volcanoes of the Chaîne des Puys. The inclined plateau to the north of the Tour-d'Auvergne also belongs to this eruptive period.
In addition, this pre-caldera volcanism produced widely differing rocks, trachytes, phonolites and rhyolites. As shown by the trachyphonolite dome of the Puy de Montcey, near Compains, formed 4 million years ago, and the rhyolitic domes of Voissière and Montmie, at Chambon-sur-Lac. The beginnings of Montdorian volcanism were also marked by phreatomagmatic eruptions, as shown by the diatreme of the Saut de la Pucelle, which was produced by the most violent eruptions of this type.

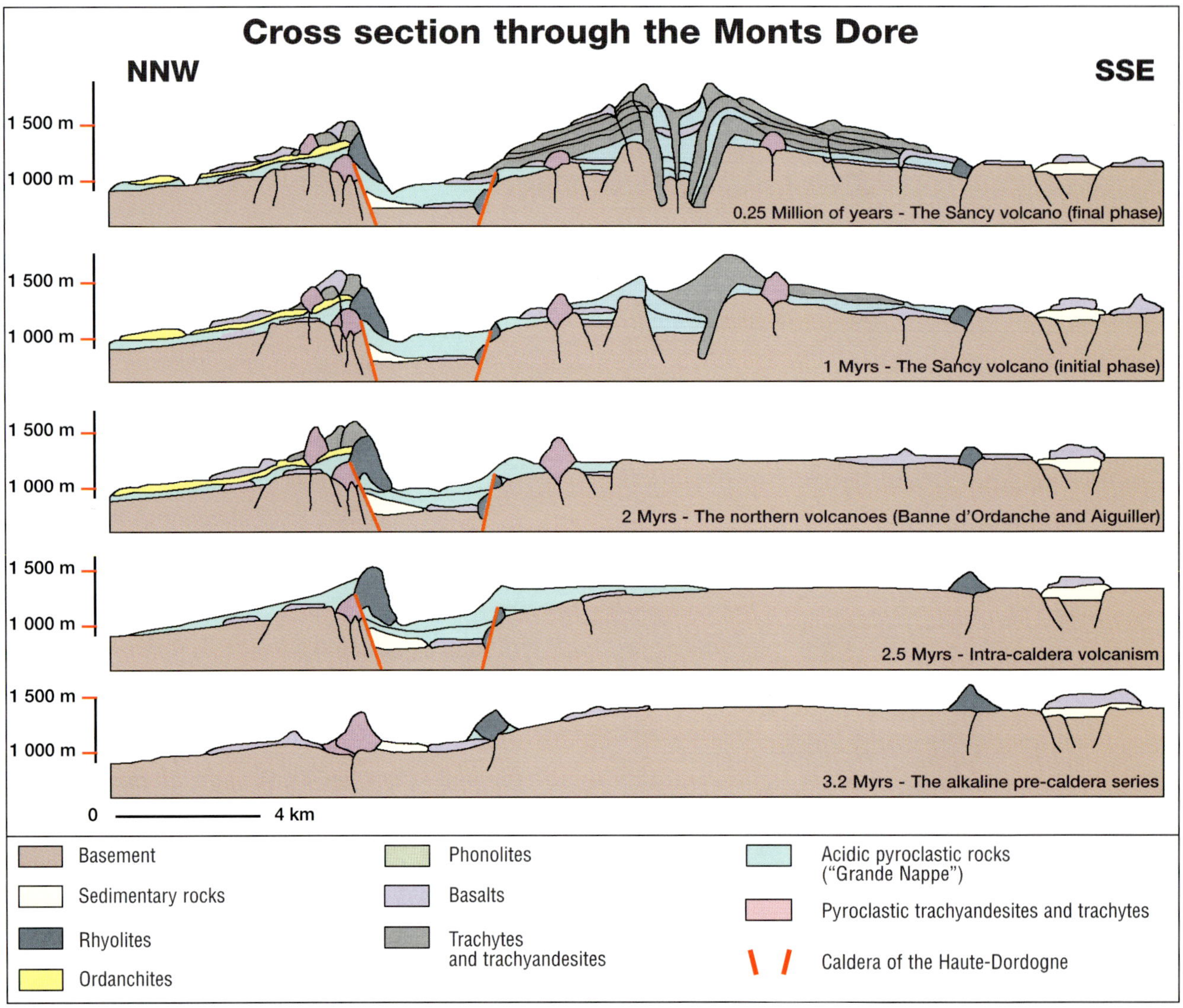

The thunderous beginnings of the strato-volcano

The birth of the Montdorian strato-volcano may be dated to 4 million years, with the formation of trachytic pumice near the massif of the Aiguiller. Then, 2.5 million years ago, an event of unparalleled magnitude in the volcanic Massif Central occurred. Fissures between La Bourboule and Le Mont-Dore ejected vast quantities of fibrous, rhyolitic pumice, known as the Grande Nappe. This eruption produced a pyroclastic flow of ash, pumice and small blocks in suspension in an aerosol at a temperature of 600°C, moving at high speed.

Above - *The castle of Murol, built on a basalt plug.*
Below - *Lake Chambon, formed by the Couze being blocked by the Tartaret, and the collapse of the Saut de la Pucelle,* on the right.

The Mont-Dore valley, between the Roc de Cuzeau and the Dôme du Capucin, follows the contours of the caldera of the Haute-Dordogne.
Inset - *Behind the Choussy hot springs at La Bourboule, one of the finest "slickensides" in Europe.*

It is for this reason that the material from this nuée ardente, which represents a volume of several cubic kilometres, spread over an area of at least 100 km², destroying everything in its path. Deposits may also be found at Saint-Nectaire-Haut, Orcival and Rochefort-Montagne.
For an idea of the magnitude of this eruption, we must look at the material produced by the Grande Nappe, formerly exploited in a quarry at the eastern entrance to Rochefort-Montagne. More than ten kilometres from the point of emission, the pumice is still more than ten metres thick!
Never has the Auvergne seen a worse volcanic eruption. It is easy to understand that the void left by this release led to the collapse of the roof of the magma chamber, thus creating the "caldera of the Haute-Dordogne", an elliptical crater with steep sides and a flat bottom, of some 20 km² and up to two hundred and fifty metres deep. Today, the caldera is difficult to see, since it has been filled by the sediments of the lake which formed in it, as well as by pyroclastic rocks from later eruptions and the collapse of its walls. Nevertheless, its northern edge may still be seen in the form of the slope which dominates the valley of the Dordogne between Le Mont-Dore and La Bourboule, where the boundary fault is still fresh behind the Choussy springs. It should be noted that the thermal water of both these spa towns rise up through fractures on the edge of the caldera.

The valley of the Dordogne at La Bourboule, with the Puy Gros on the left
Inset - *A pumice quarry at Rochefort-Montagne showing the thickness of the "Grande Nappe".*

The northern volcanoes

Post-caldera volcanic activity first took the form of acidic, silica-rich emissions, around the edge of the giant crater. Then the strato-volcano became more complex, with the expulsion of trachytic pumice, the filling of veins of trachyandesite and the formation of rhyolitic domes. These eruptions were accompanied by a series of nuées ardentes, the materials of which may be seen in the Planches quarry, to the north of La Bourboule (the C.D. 219 road). The ejecta from these volcanoes helped to fill the lake which had formed in the caldera (the cinerites which contributed to the filling contain fossil leaves and pollen).

Below - *The Roches Tuilière and Sanadoire separated by a U-shaped glacial valley.*

About 2 million years ago, extrusions of trachyphonolites occurred outside the caldera and of which the Roche Tuilière and Roche Sanadoire are their splendid remains. Between these prismatic rocks lies a typically U-shaped glacial valley: glaciation first appeared before they were formed and long cold periods occurred at the same time as the eruptions of the Monts Dore. In addition, the more discrete protrusions of the Roche Malvialle and the Puys Corde and Trioulérou may be seen in the Lake of Guéry area. At the same time, the major part of the activity of this phase, which continued until 1.6 million years ago, resulted in the formation of two complex edifices, centred around the Banne d'Ordanche (1,512 m) and the Puy de l'Aiguiller (1,525 m).

The Banne d'Ordanche is a flow of trachyandesites combined with aquagene tuffs, visible at the col de Guéry, and flows of doreites which were exuded at Laqueuille. On the slopes of the Banne d'Ordanche, the Gacherie is a rhyolitic dome-flow associated with nuées ardentes, which may be seen at the Planches quarry, whilst lower down (C.D.996), in the Monnéron quarries, a layer of pre-caldera phonolite may be seen over a trachytic dike of sancyite.

Top left - *The Puy de l'Ouire, seen from Lake of Guéry.*
Right - *The Banne d'Ordanche, which has given its name to a special form of lava, ordanchite.*
Below - *The circular shape of Lake Servières shows that it was formed by a maar.*

The highly complex Aiguiller group was the scene of, often sub-glacial, phreatomagmatic and Plinian eruptions, which eject immense plumes of trachytic pumice which cause violent storms, which in turn produce mud slides.
Far more devastating than eruptions, these lahars sweep away everything in their path and are capable of moving blocks of several hundred cubic metres. The most significant swept down as far as the Allier: at Perrier, not far from Issoire, they form an accumulation one hundred and twenty metres high. Experts think that the origin of these flows could be a lateral blast from the Aiguiller, of the type which occurred at Mount Saint-Helens in 1980.
Complex the Aiguiller group certainly is, the Puy at its centre is made up of ordanchite, the Puy de la Croix-Morand (1,519 m) is formed of a remarkable "demi-deuil" basalt and the Puy de la Tache (1,629 m) is a dome of sancyite capped with a basalt flow. In addition, these peaks are surrounded by significant deposits from the nuées ardentes they produced.

The Sancy strato-volcano

After these ragings, the Monts Dore volcano was calm for half a million years, before entering a second major phase of great activity, ten kilometres to the south of the first. The Sancy strato-volcano is an edifice dominated by trachyandesitic lava and pyroclastic rocks, with the previously mentioned variations, ordanchites and sancyites.
720,000 to 580,000 years ago, the birth of this edifice started with abundant flows of trachytic pumice. Further mud flows extended over great distances, for example those which reached the Allier near Vic-le-Comte and Coudes.
The release of such huge quantities caused the collapse of the roof of the magma chamber from which they came. Nevertheless, this second caldera, half the size of that of the Haute-Dordogne, was almost completely covered by later eruptions. At most, we may assume that the cirque at the end of the Mont-Dore valley, overlooked by the Puy de Sancy (1,886 m), is formed by part of its sides.

The cirque at the end of the Mont-Dore valley.

Above - *The Mont-Dore valley with the Capucin* on the right *and the Puy de Sancy* in the background.
Inset - *The Grande Cascade, on the edge of a thick flow of sancyite.*
Top - *The Puy de Sancy seen from the west.*
Inset - *The Aiguilles du Diable from the Fontaine Salée.*

As for the previous caldera, the evolution of this strato-volcano, which includes the highest point of Central France continued with the deposition of lake sediments of cinerite. Then, whilst basalt lava flows formed on the edge of the edifice, domes of sancyite and doreeite were formed, spewing out nuées ardentes: the Capucin (1,468 m), the Roc de Cuzeau (1,737 m), the Rocher de l'Aigle, and the Puys de la Perdrix and Barbier.

The massif was the scene of various flows, such as the Grande Cascade or the Puy de l'Angle (1,738 m). The latter is at the centre of the Massif Adventif, a distinct eruptive zone. It was here, in particular with a nuée ardente deposited on the plateau of Durbise, that the last specifically Montdorian eruptions occurred, with flows of doreite less than 250,000 years ago.

Glacial erosion then moved in to attack the volcano, exposing veins of sancyite which were formed in the middle of pyroclastic breccia. The Sancy massif is now almost Alpine in appearance, because of the exposure of dikes which form the rocks in the Val de Courre and the Chaudefour valley, including the Crète de Coq and the Dent de la Rancune.

Above - *The Chaudefour valley, bristling with dikes.*
Below left - *The Arch emerging from a dike.*
Right - *The Dent de la Rancune, the finest dike of the massif.*

Plan of the underground lake

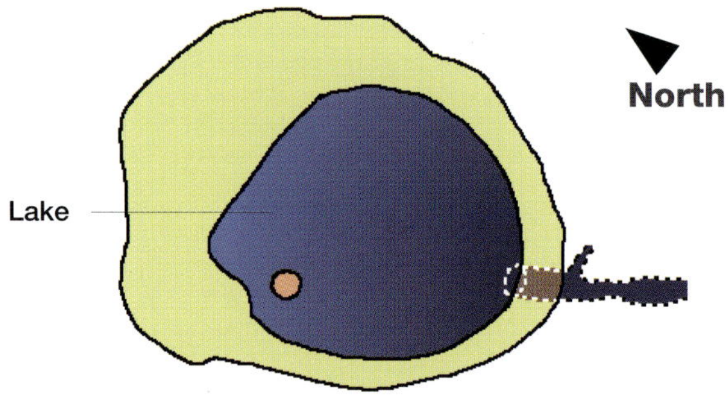

Cross section NW - SE

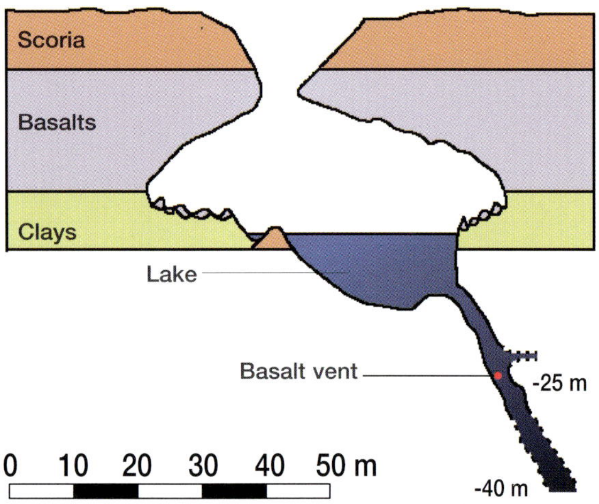

The Creux de Soucy

Hidden in woods to the south of Lake Pavin and very unexpected in a volcanic landscape, the Creux de Soucy is a gouffre (sinkhole) the narrow mouth of which, opens out into the bottom of a depression some twelve metres deep. This opening is at the apex of a cavity more than fifty metres in diameter. The bottom is filled by a lake, in which the temperature of the water is a constant 1 to 2°C. In June 1892, the first to explore the Creux de Soucy were Martel, the father of speleology, and Armand, who five years later was to discover the pot hole in the Lozère that now bears his name. The descent of these pioneers was stopped by the presence of a layer of carbonic acid.

Recent explorations have shown that, given the nature of the rocks and the shaft that plunges almost vertically in the bottom of the lake, the Creux de Soucy could be a secondary vent from the Puy de Montchal which formed a pocket of gas under a flow as it cooled.

Formation of a maar

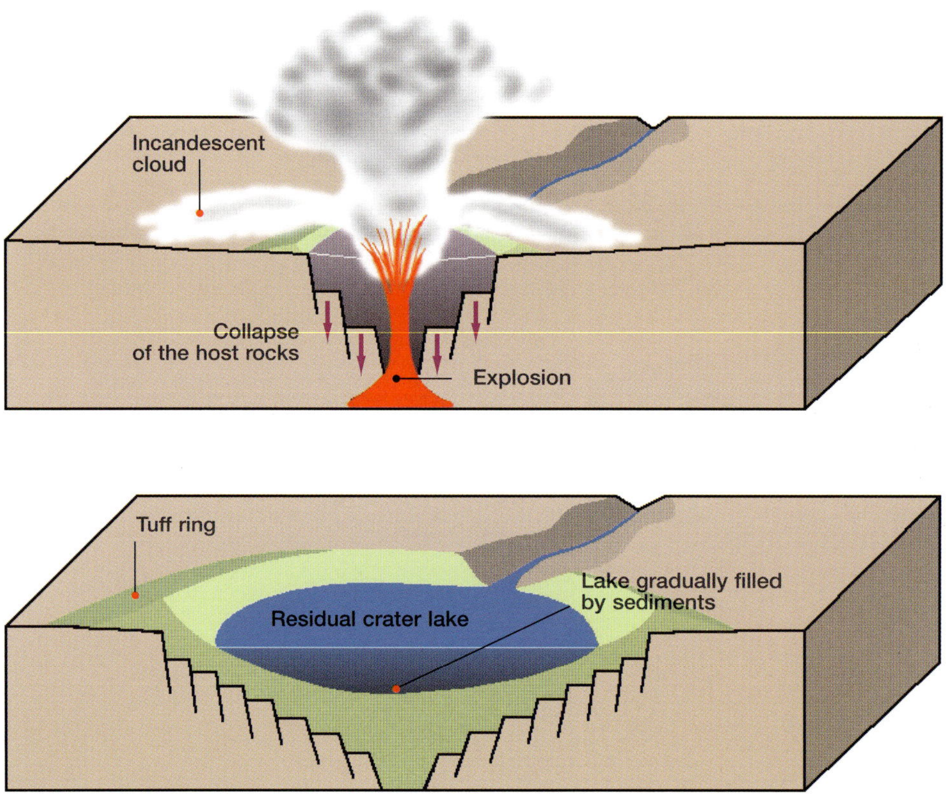

Young dispersed volcanoes

Like that which occurred in the far reaches of the Cézalier with the Montchal and Pavin group, recent volcanoes, distant cousins of those of the Chaîne des Puys, rose on the edge of the Monts Dore massif, to the north and east, for example the Puy de Vivanson, to the north of the Banne d'Ordanche. Dispersed cinder cones, lava flows and maars complete the landscapes formed by the old strato-volcano. Particularly remarkable is the Tartaret, which erupted in a valley bottom, which it blocked to form Lake Chambon and a long flow from which flowed into the couze. The maar of the Lake Servières also belongs to this period of volcanic activity of less than 100,000 years ago.

Above - *Lake Pavin, a maar of more than 90 metres deep, overlooked by the fine crater of the Puy de Montchal.*
Below - *Lake Chambon, with the volcano of the Tartaret on the left, which blocked the "couze".*

The Cézalier, a basalt cap, includes several outstanding edifices, such as the Mont Chamaroux, with the Monts Dore and the Puy de Dôme in the distance.

The Cézalier

The Cézalier is a high basalt plateau which separates the Monts Dore and the Cantal. This 600 km^2 sheet of lava, is separated from the former by the valley of the Couze Pavin and from the second by an indeterminate area, between Allanche and the Allagnon valley, where its lava flows mix with those of the planezes.
Perched on a horst in the gneiss basement, the Cézalier rises to a height of 1,551 metres at the Signal du Luguet and has two of the highest villages in the Auvergne, Montgreleix (1,231 m) and La Godivelle (1,203 m). Despite its gentle form, the Cézalier is a complex volcano, like is great neighbours, between which it fits chronologically.
Apart from early signs dating back 20 million years, on the edge of the Artense, eruptions began 8 million years ago with stacks of basalt and ended three million years later. A small strato-volcano was formed near Boutaresse. This Cantal in miniature combines maars, masses of volcanic breccia, domes and thick lava flows, together with fallback deposits and pyroclastic flows of ash and pumice.

Rivers of basalt

However, this edifice is only visible in the valleys which start to the north-west of the Signal du Luguet. Since, in the Pliocene era, a new phase of eruption of highly fluid basalts began and continued for two million years. Then, the glaciers of the Quaternary period wore down the heights of the massif and eruptions occurred sporadically on the eastern edge of the plateau.
They produced basaltic, cinder cone volcanoes, with lava flows which fossilised the valleys running towards the Alagnon and the Allier. They are mainly the Malnon, Chapel-Marcousse, Zanières, Mazoires and Autrac volcanoes. A large number of sites beside the Alagnon, provide examples of this

Near Besse, the Jarrige plateau and the valley of the Vaucoux.
Inset - *The Signal du Luguet.*

The Allagnon valley, near Massiac, framed by two cliffs carved out of lava flows from the Cézalier.
Inset - *The chapel Sainte-Madeleine, on the east cliff.*
Below - *The Rentières valley, up-river of Ardes, where the couze has dug into the side of a basalt flow.*

Formation of an inverted flow

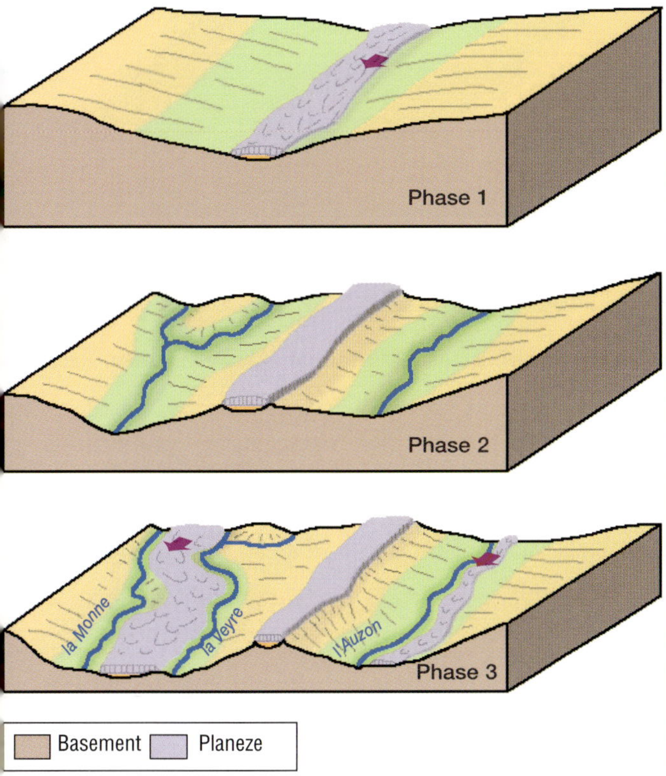

form of volcanism, such as the prismatic cliff on which is perched the chapel to Sainte-Madeleine, at Massiac.

The same is true in the Pays Coupé, where the couzes have inverted the lava flows, thus revealing the terraces of the Rentières valley and the fine tables of the Lembron, opposite the last volcanic outcrops of the Limagne.

The recent eruptions in the Cézalier, include that which formed the crater Lake of La Godivelle-d'en-Haut, 110,000 years ago. Its circular shape and depth, 45 metres, prove that it was formed by a maar, whilst the Lake of La Godivelle d'en-Bas, which is shallow and surrounded by peat bogs, is a typical glacial depression. This area, blunted by ice ages, also features the fine cinder cone of the Chamaroux (1,476 m) and the volcano of Montgreleix (1,281 m), some 160,000 years old. The lava flows of the falls of Entraigues, which are thought to be from the Puy de la Vaisse, are a mere 50,000 years old. Note the small, little known maar of La Fage, at the source of the stream.

Above - *The twin Lakes of La Godivelle: that of La Godivelle d'en-Haut occupies the crater of a maar, whilst that of La Godivelle d'en-Bas is the result of overdeepening.*
Below left - *The falls of Egliseneuve-d'Entraigues.* Below right - *The small maar of La Fage.*

The last fires in the Massif Central

Further to the north, Lake of Bourdouze and the Chambedaze peat bog are glacial in origin, unlike Lake Chauvet, which at 70 metres deep, is a splendid maar formed during the last ice age. This area, on the fringes of the Cézalier and the Monts Dore, was the scene of the final convulsions of the Massif Central, which saw four or five eruptions in less than two centuries, about 7,000 years ago.
This activity began with the formation of the Montcineyre, a volcano consisting of a breached cone of black ash, the lava from which flowed into the couze de Valbeleix to the village of the same name. This cinder cone blocked a stream which formed a lake around the side of the volcano, with a beach littered with shiny black crystals of pyroxene.

The second event was the explosion of the maar of Estivadoux, now filled, as witnessed by the still thick layer of bedded tuff and a small lake. Then, the Puy de Montchal and its crater formed on the edge of this lake. This eruption combined scoria ejecta with an abundant flow of trachybasalt down the valley of the Couze Pavin to the edge of the village of Saurier.
Finally, at the foot of the Montchal, a very violent explosion of the maar type produced Lake Pavin, which is more than 90 metres deep. This volcanic group therefore represents a complete magmatic cycle, which is thought to be due to the emptying of a small magma chamber close to the surface.

Above - *Lake Chauvet, one of the most recent maars of the Massif Central.*
Below - *Lake of Montcineyre, before the dam formed by the volcano of the same name.*

The lines of crests which form a star at the centre of the Massif Cantal show how glaciers have dismantled this enormous volcano.

The Monts du Cantal

A "titanic volcano with a hundred heads", the Cantal is a colossus with thousands of vents from which the planezes formed twenty arms... It covers 2,500 km^2, that is two and half times the area of Etna, which makes the Cantal the largest volcanic edifice in Europe and one of the most complex anywhere. But the Cantal is totally dead, it became extinct some 3 million years ago. Here there are no craters and what we can see today is the skeleton of a strato-volcano, the genesis of which is still not fully understood. Geologists first thought that in its youth the Massif Cantal, today a low cone, rose to a height of 3,500 metres. This figure was then reduced, but more recently, in the light of the eruption of Mount Saint-Helens in 1980, it would appear that the figure proposed by the scientists of the 19th century was probable accurate. On the other hand, the destructive processes were very different from that which had been assumed for a very long time.

A genesis still not fully understood

Before the appearance of the volcanoes, was the ancient basement, the heir of the great Hercynian chain worn down by erosion. 30 million years ago, the folding of the Alps and other movements of the Earth's crust fractured this basement of granites and metamorphic rocks: basins formed in the collapsed areas to be filled by alluvium from raised blocks which had been eroded.
The Margeride is a model for such raised blocks, whilst its rifts remain in the form of the depressions of Saint-Flour and Aurillac. Under the heart of the Cantal lies another of these collapses, bounded by faults that form a polygon which, for some time, led experts to think that it was a caldera.

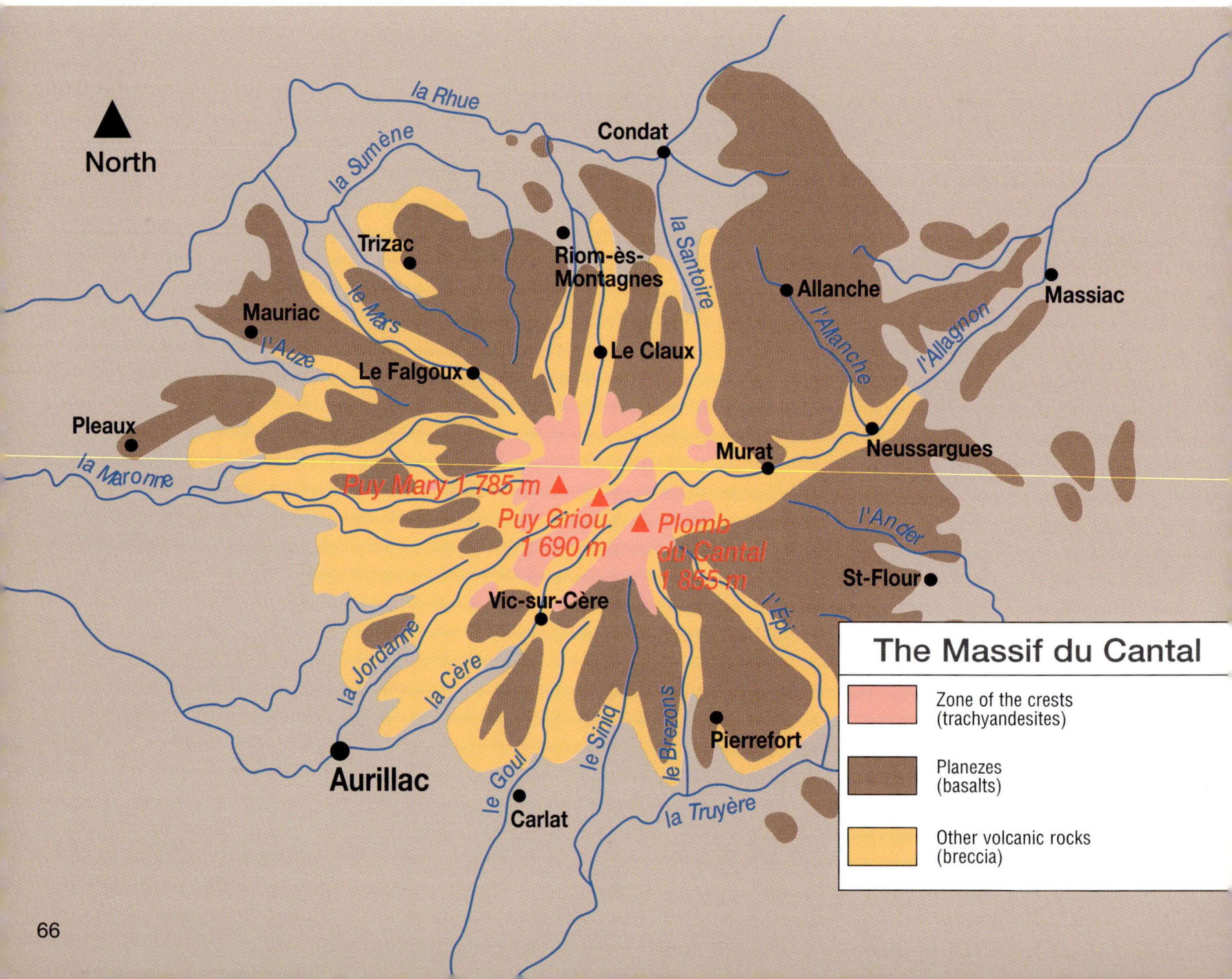

The protrusions of the Griou and the Grionot.
Inset - *The Claux valley and the pyramidal peak of Puy Mary.*
Below - *The eastern flank of Puy Mary, from which opens out the Brèche de Roland.*

The first basalts

Such is the context in which the first, sporadic eruptions occurred in the massif, 13 to 11 million years ago. Later covered, these basalts remain visible on the edges of the Cantal and in certain valley floors, where they have been exposed. To the north of the volcano, one of the most ancient flows is found near Condat, on the banks of the Santoire. The high valleys of the Petite Rhue, the Véronne and the Allagnon, between Laveissière and Murat, also reveal these "pre-Cantalian" basalts. Eruptions of this type, accompanied by emissions of phreatomagmatic tuffs and scoria ejecta, occurred up to 7 million years ago, at the time the strato-volcano was being formed. Their products appear on the edge of the massif, in the form of "pericantalian" basalts and form certain features in the Jordanne valley, up-river from Aurillac, and in the Ander valley, near Saint-Flour.

Thiézac, in the Cere valley, overlooked by basalt rocks dating from the beginning of the formation of the Cantalian volcano.

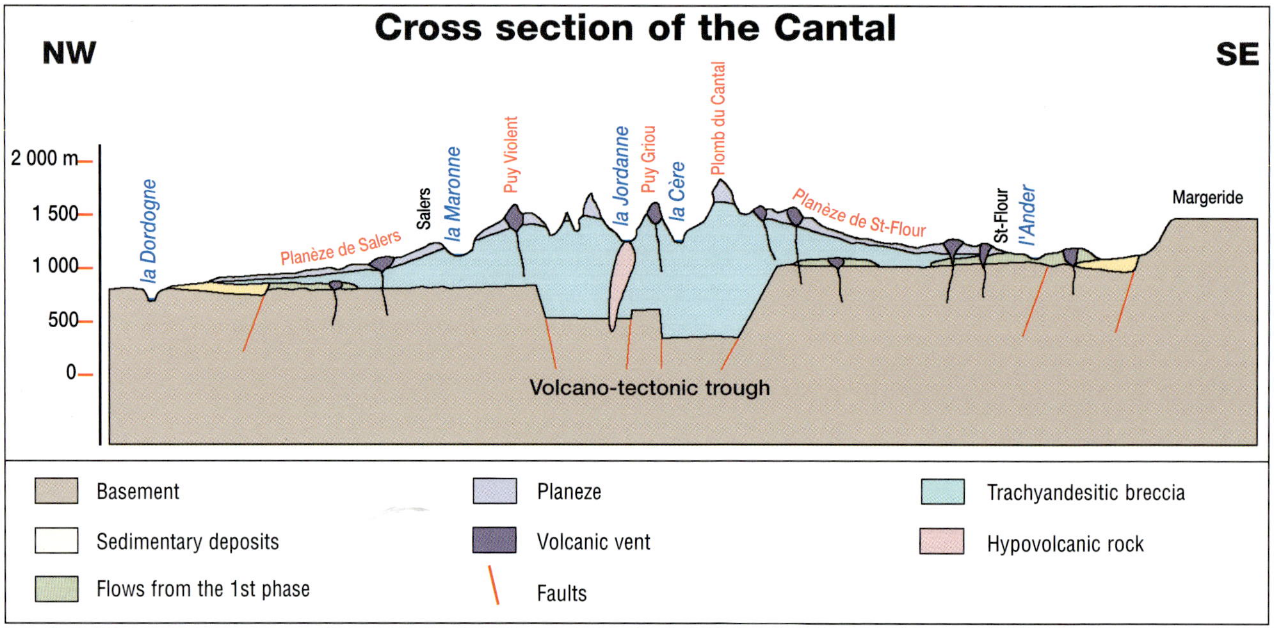

A strato-volcano, built up and destroyed several times

The lavas of this initial phase are alkali basalts and basanites which evolve to become hawaiites, proof of the gradual formation of a deep magma chamber. The strato-volcano of the Cantal was formed from this chamber during an agitated period, which lasted between 9 to 6.5 million years ago, by the viscous magma that caused particularly explosive eruptions, interspersed with long dormant periods. At the heart of the Cantal, dozens of vents became active, only some of which are identifiable as peaks. Beside these crests in the central part of the massif, made up of the remains of lava flows and domes, most of the Cantal is made up of pyroclastic rocks ejected by explosions at the end of the Miocene epoch. The natural bowls formed by the great valleys give us some idea of their abundance, which is estimated at 80% of the total volume.

Above - *The Mandailles valley.*
Below - *This view shows the complexity of the strato-volcano of the Cantal with, in line, the Puy de la Tourte, Puy Mary, the Peyre-Arse, Puy Griou and the Plomb du Cantal.*

The riches of the volcanic sub-soil of the Cantal.

The Cantal has developed the exploitation of basalt, once a building stone and which is now crushed for road surfacing. Near Riom-ès-Montagnes, two quarries in the trachytic domes of Augoules and Meynoire supply the region with pale dressed stone. In the past, the edge of the planeze of Saint-Flour was known for the extraction of Bouzentès stone. This stone which is very similar to Volvic stone, a basalt full of pores, was used for centuries in the eastern part of the massif, in particular for the Saint-Flour cathedral. Between Murat and Dienne, the lauzières (roofing stone quarries) of the col d'Entremont supplied the area with roofing stones for covering buildings, until the use of slate became common more recently. These roofing stones were a light grey trachyandesite, which is still one of the features of the roofs of the old town of Murat. Certain buildings in this town have walls built with stacked sections of basalt columns taken from the Rocher de Bonnevie which overlooks the town. The diatomites of Murat (Sainte-Reine-Faufouilloux) and Riom-ès-Montagnes (Collandre-la-Bade), were marketed under the name of "silica". This material was not produced by volcanic activity but is an indirect result of it; it was formed by the accumulation of the siliceous skeletons of minute planktonic algae, which developed in the deep lakes of the maars.

Volcanic roofing stones covering the church of Chastel-sur-Murat.
Inset - *A barn near Messilhac the walls and the roof of which show the diversity of the volcanic materials of the Cantal.*

The meanders of the Truyère cutting through certain lava flows in the south of the Cantal.
Inset - *Near Murat, a deposit of ejecta folded by a landslide.*

A series of cataclysms

The experts were at pains to understand the superimposition of ash, pumice, ignimbrites, lahars, breccia and conglomerates, until the eruption of Mount Saint-Helens, on the 18th May 1980, opened up new ways for volcanology. It was then understood that the deposits in the Cantal are not all due directly to an eruptive phase: most were reformed by lateral blasts which saw considerable parts of the primitive cone collapse. At least three cataclysmic eruptions of this type devastated the Cantal, by carrying off and pulverising vast quantities of materials.
Firstly trachyrhyolitic, the Cantal collapsed towards Aurillac and Vic-sur-Cère 8.5 million years ago. Rebuilt of trachyandesitic materials, the volcano exploded to the north-west 7.5 million years ago. Finally, a third edifice to the south was torn apart 6.5 million years ago, as revealed by the materials covering the flows of the Aubrac to the south of the Truyère.
The great valleys in the west show the wide range of materials produced by these cataclysms. The avalanches of debris can be seen upstream by the slippage of plates en masse. Further down, these valleys reveal flows of debris, at Marmanhac and Velzic. Finally, near Aurillac mud flows appear; they are lahars rich in blocks and poor in pumice, associated with this special type of eruption, the lateral blast.

The Plomb du Cantal, and inset, *its small cap rising above the crests, the remains of an ancient lava lake.*

The basalts of the plateaux

It is on these ruins, around which the gentle slope retained its original conical shape, that a third phase of activity started after the central magma chamber was drained. Following the differentiated lavas, various types of fluid basalt flow were again laid down on the edge of the strato-volcano, from 6 to 4 million years ago.
The most abundant flows formed the magnificent Saint-Flour planeze. These Supracantalian basalt flows from a large number of peripheral fissures, formed other planezes throughout the massif. This activity occurred as far as the Xaintrie in the Corrèze and the abundance of the flows is particularly visible in Puy Violent, where the lava flows piled up to a thickness of two hundred and fifty metres. Occasionally, the traces of cinder cones from this period may be seen, such as the one at Tanavelle, near Saint-Flour.

Puy Violent and the crest line leading to Puy Mary.
Inset - *"Square columns" near Chalinargues.*
Below - *The low cinder cone at Tanavelle, on the Saint-Flour planeze.*

Murat with the necks at Bredons, Bonnevie and Chastel-sur-Murat.
Inset - *The neck at Chastel-sur-Murat with its chapel.*

Later occurrences produced the necks which surround Murat for example, whilst the Plomb du Cantal, which was formed 3 million years ago, marked the end of activity in the massif. The exposure of these landforms underlines the extent of the erosion to which the Cantal was subjected, particularly during the last Ice Age, which ended 10,000 years ago. Signs of such erosive action may be seen in U-shaped valleys which radiate in a star shape from the centre of the Cantal and highlight the planezes, the moraines of the plateaux, raised basalt plugs and pyramidal "horn" peaks, such as Puy Mary.

The typically U-shaped glacial Brezons valley.

The Tranchades de Laquairie

Near Condat, the Tranchades de Laquairie is a remarkable volcanic site. This is a basalt flow some 4.5 million years old, which covered scoria which had been deposited on a thin layer of clay on the gneiss basement. First inverted by erosion, the edge of the prismatic flow was then driven downward by the slippage of the underlying clays, thus forming crevasses 20 metres deep (below). The vegetation on this site, which is encouraged by the humid conditions, is reminiscent of tropical climes (below). The Tranchades are also the scene of a rare phenomenon, since they contain ice holes, like those in the Chaîne des Puys. In these cavities, ice forms even in summer. Not far away, one can also see the Roche pointue, a neck exposed by the Santoire with its crown of breccia riddled with bands of aragonite that culminate in a bouquet of needles (opposite).

At the heart of the massif

One of the important sites of the Haute Auvergne, one of the accesses to which is blocked by snow for half the year, the Pas de Peyrol (1,582 m) is an impressive balcony overlooking the Cantal. Even better, the nearby peak of Puy Mary (1,787 m), which may be reached in half an hour, quite simply provides one of the most magnificent views in the whole of France. These grandiose landscapes owe much to the action of glaciers which carved out cirques and steep sided U-shaped valleys. Carved into a pyramidal peak by the intersection of four glacial cirques, Puy Mary is the remains of a Pelean dome, the rock of which is similar to the sancyites of the Monts Dore. At the bottom of the access road, the car park is excavated in the breccia of nuées ardentes ejected by the volcano. The peaks around this giant also represent the past furies of the Cantal.

Above - *The majestic pyramidal peak of Puy Mary seen from the north, from the rocks close to the Pas de Peyrol.*
Below - *The south-east face of Puy Mary and the cirque of the Impradine.*

These crests are trachyandesitic, in particular the Chavaroche, the Peyre-Arse and the Roc des Ombres. In the distance, one can see the basalt plug of the peak of the Plomb du Cantal (1,855 m) and, nearer, phonilite pitons, of which Puy Griou (1,690 m) is the model. The shape and colour of the peaks in this family, such as the Griounot and Usclade in the Mandailles valley, are characteristic. Several exposed veins, such as the dike on the flank of the Chapeloune, are of this type. The Roc d'Hozières is also a protrusion of phonolite and comparable landforms extend off into the distance as far as the columns at Bort, the final extension of volcanism in the Cantal in this direction.

Above - *The front of columns at Bort.*
Below - *The Roc d'Hozières and the Roche Taillade, on the crest leading from Puy Mary to Puy Violent.*

Above left - *The Brèche de Roland.* right - *The block of phonolite of Puy Griou.*
Inset - *The Griounot.*

Below and also inset - *The Peyre-Arse.*

The neck at Laqueuille, opposite Dienne in the Santoire valley.
Inset - *Near Allanche, lateritic soil of African appearance, which is evidence of a period of tropical climate, was covered and baked by a basalt flow.*

From planezes to valleys

Around these peaks, varied outcrops are a delight for geology lovers, from the gabbros of the Mandailles valley to the fumarole induced alterations of the Rhue de Cheylade. Apart from these curiosities, the list of the volcanic riches of the Cantal continues on the fringe of the peaks with a host of rocky sites, where basalt may be seen in all its forms. The planezes are marked by several escarpments, for example; the basanite neck of Laqueille which lies near Dienne, or the black rock on which the castle of Apchon is built. It is on the edge of the plateaux that the most remarkable basalt features may be seen. There, the rivers have exposed lava flows, which often take the form of columns.

The site of Apchon, with the neck of the ancient castle and a small plateau formed by a flow.

The Table de Carlat is a flow exposed by erosion.
Inset - *The columns of Le Roudadou.*

Upper Saint-Flour, on a plateau ringed with basalt columns.
Inset - *The Salins falls, near Mauriac.*

The admirable columns of Le Roudadou, the most regular in the massif, and the impressive dimensions of the famous Table of Carlat are found here. Some of these prismatic features are magnified by water falls, such as the Faillitoux falls, near Thiézac, the Salins falls, not far from Mauriac, where the Auze passes over a lip some thirty metres high and the Saillant falls, where the Ander passes over the Saint-Flour flow.

In the valleys, rise fine basalt plugs, such as the Rocher de Bonnevie and the Rocher de Bredons at Murat, outcrops associated with the neck of porphyritic basalt, which overlooks Chastel-sur-Murat. Several superimposed layers separating scoria may also be seen, such as the Suc de Rome, in the Véronne valley. The imposing prismatic rock of Chastel-Merlhac is evidence of a former lava lake, like that of Laval, at Neussargues.

The "giant's causeway" of the Pont des Nègres.

« C'est comme un morceau de continent chauve et brusquement exondé qui ferait surface au-dessus des sempiternelles campagnes bocagères qui sont la banalité de notre terroir. »
Julien Gracq

The Aubrac

« On peut garder de grands souvenirs de l'Aubrac. Tant d'air passe sur ces pâturages où se débandent de loin en loin trois arbres et où il y a tant de ciel. »

Henri Pourrat

Before discussing the Aubrac massif, which is detached from the Cantal complex, we must mention other, isolated examples of volcanic activity covering small, scarcely noticeable areas, around the Truyère, near the famous Garabit viaduct. Sitting astride the departments of the Cantal, the Aveyron and the Lozère, the volcanic part of the Aubrac is a rump, some four to eight kilometres wide and some forty kilometres long, running north-west to south-east, along the main fault lines of the eastern part of the Massif Central.

Two blocks, on either side of this basement fracture, have moved: to the south, the western block sank 200 to 300 metres, which resulted in its northern part being raised above the western block, near the Truyère. The Aubrac is transversely asymmetrical, with slight slopes to the east and a pronounced scar to the west. The highest point of this area, the altitude of which is generally in excess of 1,000 metres is the Signal de Mailhebiau (1,469 m), which along with the Puy du Roussillon (1,408 m) and the Roc du Cayla (1,298 m) lie along the main fracture.

Top left - *The expanses of the Aubrac with the Puy de Roussillon in the distance.*
Right - *The Roc du Cayla, near Laguiole.*
Bottom - *The Bès stream between Saint-Urcize and La Chaldette, the waters of which have exposed a small neck,* also inset.

A volcanic cap worn down by glaciers

The Aubrac was formed during a few brief episodes over approximately two million years, at the end of the Miocene epoch. The driving force was first Strombolian, to judge by the mass of ejecta which are still visible, particularly to the west of the Signal de Malhebiau. Then, abundant basalt flows, sometimes mixed with ash, known as "lava tuff", covered these edifices, often superimposing each other, such as the twenty odd lava flows on top of each other at the Truques d'Aubrac. Most of the gently undulating peaks of the Aubrac, locally known as "trucs", are flows of this type which have been worn down by glaciers. The high average altitude of the massif meant that the glaciers of the Quaternary period formed a cap. The highly friable nature of the basalts in the Aubrac may be seen in the considerable moraine deposits which cover the granite peneplain to the east of the massif, whilst the series of lakes and peat bogs which scatter the landscape to the south-east of Nasbinals, are evidence of the overdeepening of these ice ages.

Above - *The Lake of Saint-Andéol, of glacial origin.*
Below - *The Signal de Malhebiau and the vast expanses of the Aubrac, a cap worn down by glaciers.*
Inset - *One of the erratics left by the glaciers of the Quaternary period.*

Lake of Born, in the middle of the famous pastures of the Aubrac.
Inset - *A buron with its paddock of blocks of basalt*

The volcanic nature of the Aubrac is only clear in the harder flows, such as the basalts of Saint-Urcize, which have been carved into an overdeepened cirque. To the west of the massif, the steepness of the slopes also favoured the erosion of cradle valleys, with cirques at their head, such as that at Saint-Chély-d'Aubrac. Further down to the west, as to the north of Laguiole, the streams were powerful enough to invert the flows, particularly in the Boraldes area, where they flow into the Lot. Two famous volcanic sites prove the origin of the Aubrac; the Déroc falls, where the Bès flows over the edge of a high flow, and the Pont des Nègres, which is a "giant's causeway" of human dimensions, which provides a fording point on the Plèches stream.

Below - *The Saint-Urcize cirque, evidence of glacial erosion.* Inset - *The Bes plateau.*
Opposite centre - *The Rocher de Belvezet, near Saint-Chély-d'Aubrac*
Bottom - *The Déroc falls, which flow over the front of a prismatic flow.*

Marchastel nestles at the bottom of a basalt dike and several outcrops of the same type rise above Lake of Born. In the Boraldes, where basaltic, often prismatic rocks abound, geologists will appreciate an outcrop of breccia, scoria, bombs and cinerites, near Linars. On the other side of the Lot, stand the isolated buttes at Roquelaure and Calmont-d'Olt.

Above - *The dike at Marchastel.*
Below top - *The picturesque town Roquelaure, with its mediaeval towers and volcanic rocks.*
Bottom - *Above Espalion, the basalt butte of the castle at Calmont.*

Chaudes-Aigues and the Chateau du Couffour.
Inset - *The Par hot springs, at a temperature of 82°C.*

Chaudes-Aigues, the beginnings of geothermy

Although there is no direct relationship between volcanism and hot springs, Chaudes-Aigues has its place in this work, so aware is the town that its hot springs are evidence of the "fire burning in the bowels of the earth".
Nevertheless, volcanism and thermalism have one thing in common, that is the existence of a network of open fractures linking the surface with the depths. Le Mont-Dore and La Bourboule combine a volcanic edifice with the rise of hot springs. This is not the case at Chaudes-Aigues, which has the hottest waters in Europe, as shown by the Par spring, which provides 300 litres a minute at a temperature of 82°C.
The mechanism at the origin of these spectacular discharges is the thermosiphon. Rain water, partially absorbed by small fissures, filters down to a depth of several kilometres and is heated by a higher than average geothermal gradient. This high temperature (about 200°C) is the cause of the upwelling of water, which is now lighter. The phenomenon is accentuated, since the waters are charged with carbon dioxide, the main gas in the Earth's crust and which also forms most volcanic gases.
This gas escapes as the water emerges, resulting in the deposit of less soluble elements, with which it was charged. They are mainly carbonates of lime, which form needles of aragonite and crystals of calcite, stained with rust from traces of iron hydroxides. Eventually, these deposits block the pipes that heat the houses of Chaudes-Aigues.

The castle at Polignac, only the keep of which remains, used the natural defences provided by a tabular volcano of the Surtsey type.

The Devès and the basin of Le Puy-en-Velay

Volcanic activity in the Velay covers the southern half of the Haute-Loire and spills out on to the high plateau of the Ardèche. It is dispersed into three, very different groups, the Devès, the Le Puy basin and the Chaîne du Meygal-Mézenc. Formed on a highly erratic underlying crystalline layer, this volcanism is organised along a network of faults running north-west to south-east, bisected by perpendicular fractures. It differs in the nature of its lavas, which are virtually all alkaline. The often original manifestations of such telluric activities, give these regions a character all of their own; from the unforgettable rocks at Le Puy-en-Velay to the Sucs of the Haut-Velay, including the famous Gerbier de Jonc.

The Devès, between the Loire and the Allier

Less spectacular, the Devès nevertheless holds some surprises. With its 850 km^2, this range of highlands between the Loire and the Allier is the largest basaltic plateau in France. These flows are from the eruption of more than one hundred and fifty Strombolian volcanoes, the highest of which is Mont Devès, at 1,421 metres, whilst the landscape is scattered with more than fifty maars.

At Saint-Arcons-d'Allier, an astonishing example of the use of basalt columns in a building.

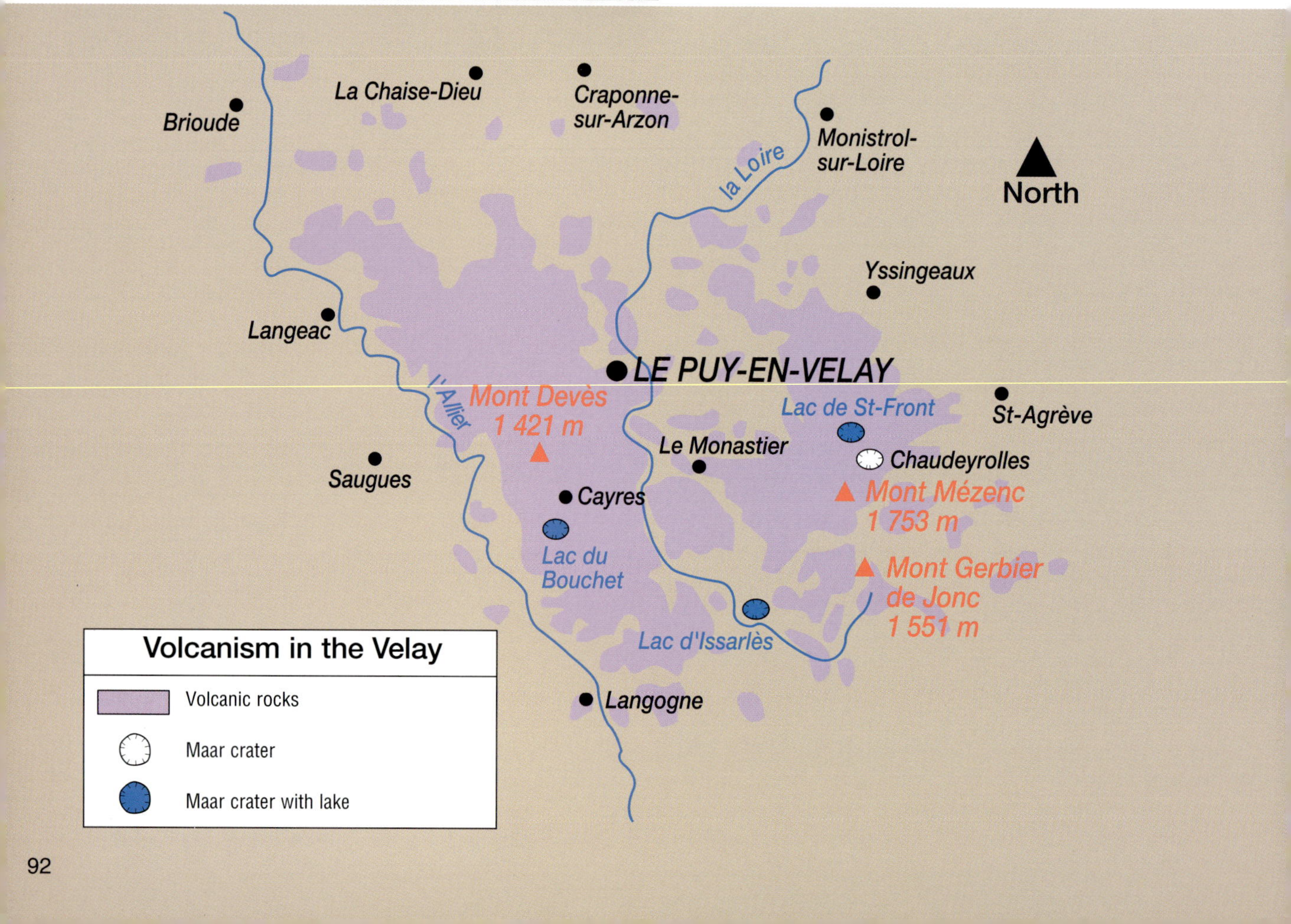

The great age of the Devès has allowed erosion to wear down the relief of its cinder cones, which are known as "gardes" here. Therefore, the only crater still worthy of note in the massif is Mont Bar, near Allègre. It is filled by a peat bog, which is highly unusual for a Strombolian volcano.

Above - *Le Puy-en-Velay where the chapel of Saint-Michel d'Aiguilhe, the statue of Notre-Dame de France and the cathedral are built on three different volcanoes.*
Below - *The peat bog of the crater of Mont Bar.*

Similarly, the maars are filled to a greater or lesser extent, such as those in the Limagne marshes, near Saint-Jean-de-Nay, or the Narse of La Sauvetat. The maar filled by the superb Lake of Le Bouchet, with a diameter of 750 metres and a depth of 28 metres, is a noteworthy exception. The volcanoes of the Devès are aligned and sometimes side by side in the highest part of the plateau, not far from the Allier, since the basement is unsymmetrical and drops away quickly in the west to form a series of steps towards Le Puy-en-Velay.
As with the main fault, these secondary fractures were the origin of abundant flows of highly fluid basalts. Volcanic activity in the Devès began

Above - *The Limagne marshes, near Saint-Jean-de-Nay.*
Below - *The Narse of La Sauvetat.* Inset - *The peaty soil of the Narse.*

3 million years ago with abundant flows of basalt. These flows fossilised the existing relief, including the deep valleys of the tributaries of the Allier. In the gorges of this river, at Prades, Saint-Arcons, Chanteuges and Chilhac, one may admire prismatic columns which are among the most remarkable of the Massif Central. On the other hand, towards the Loire, the flows are raised after having been inverted by erosion.

Above top - *Lake of Le Bouchet, formed by a maar.*
Bottom - *The astonishing prismatic formation at Chilhac, with an isolated block bearing a cross.*

Volcanic activity in this region became more explosive, hence the appearance of cinder cones, and, on the main fault line, a dozen maars. Most eruptions occurred between 1.8 and 0.7 million years ago, and activity continued at the approaches of the Loire. The "gardes" of the Devès are interesting for the immense panoramas that the highest offer, such as the Durande, and, where a "pozzolana" quarry has opened their sides, such as Mont Briançon, the assorted scoria includes spindle or cauliflower shaped volcanic bombs.

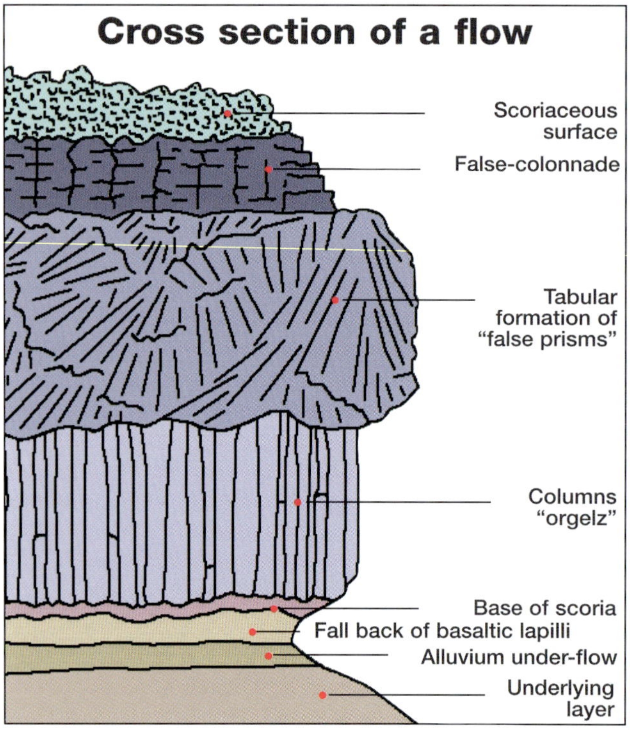

Underwater volcanism in the Le Puy basin

The basin of Le Puy-en-Velay is a fault trough between two raised blocks of granite. This depression was filled by lakes at the turn of the Tertiary and Quaternary periods. It was when they arrived at the surface in this context, that basalts produced such unusual eruptions in the Massif Central. They are known as Surtseyan, in reference to the eruption on the Icelandic island of Surtsey in 1963, which showed us what happens when fluid magma comes into contact with an abundant but relatively thin body of water.

In this case, the vaporisation of water makes the eruption explosive but, unlike maars, they are relatively limited explosions, which follow each other at brief intervals.

They produce a high column of steam charged with ash and eject black plumes heavily charged with ash, lapilli and bombs, several hundreds of metres in the air. These plumes construct tuff cones with wide craters, the centre of which is consolidated by pyroclastic rocks made up of a yellowy, glassy material which cements the very black, angular basaltic debris. These are known as palagonite breccia.

This exceptional type of eruption (which is only found elsewhere around the Puy de l'Ouire in the Monts Dore, near Saint-Flour and in the Santoire valley) is almost the rule in the Le Puy-en-Velay basin. Erosion has carried off the soft sediments and ash which surrounded these edifices, but their breccia vents remains standing, particularly where they are reinforced with veins of basalt.

Above - *Le Puy-en-Velay and its original form of volcanism, in a fault trough.*
Opposite top - *The abbey church of Chanteuges, on one of the many flows which end in the valley of the Allier.* Centre - *The imposing rocks of Prades.*
Bottom - *Saint-Ilpize, with the basalt rock on which the castle chapel was built.*

Top - *The Rocher d'Aiguilhe and the Rocher Corneille with, in the foreground, a wall on the banks of the Borne built with the columns from Espaly.*
Inset - *The cathedral and the Virgin Mary, which have volcanic bases.*
Above - *Ceyrac, dominated by the ring of a Surtsey type volcano.*
Left - *Plumes of columns at Servissac.*

Such is the origin of the extraordinary site of Le Puy, where the old volcanoes have left the necks of the Rocher Saint-Michel d'Aiguilhe, the Rocher Corneille and the Mont Anis, hidden under the cathedral and its outbuildings. This monument was partially constructed of palagonite breccia from the quarries of Chaspuzac. Other evidence of the Surtsey type eruptions of the Le Puy basin remains in the form of rocks, at Bilhac for example, but also in the form of low circular ramparts, such as the volcano at Cheyrac, or tabular landforms such as that on which the famous castle at Polignac was built.

This form of volcanism ended between 1.5 and 2 million years ago, when the plain dried out, leaving the way for more normal activity, comparable to that of the "gardes" and maars of the Devès. This evolution may be seen by examining Mont Denise, at the gates of Le Puy: the quarries in its sides reveal a basement of palagonite breccia, under a cinder cone and basaltic bombs. The maars are grouped near Saint-Paulien. The last eruptions occurred a million years go to the south of the basin, in the Loire valley.

Above - *Mont Denise, with a pozzolana quarry, above the columns at Espaly, with Polignac in the distance.*
Below - *The sharpest neck in the Auvergne, the Rocher d'Aiguilhe, which rises to a height of 80 metres.*

The Cirque des Boutières seen from Saint-Clément with, in the background, the Gerbier de Jonc on the left *and the Mont Mézenc* on the right.

The Emblavès, the Haut-Velay and the Ardèche mountains

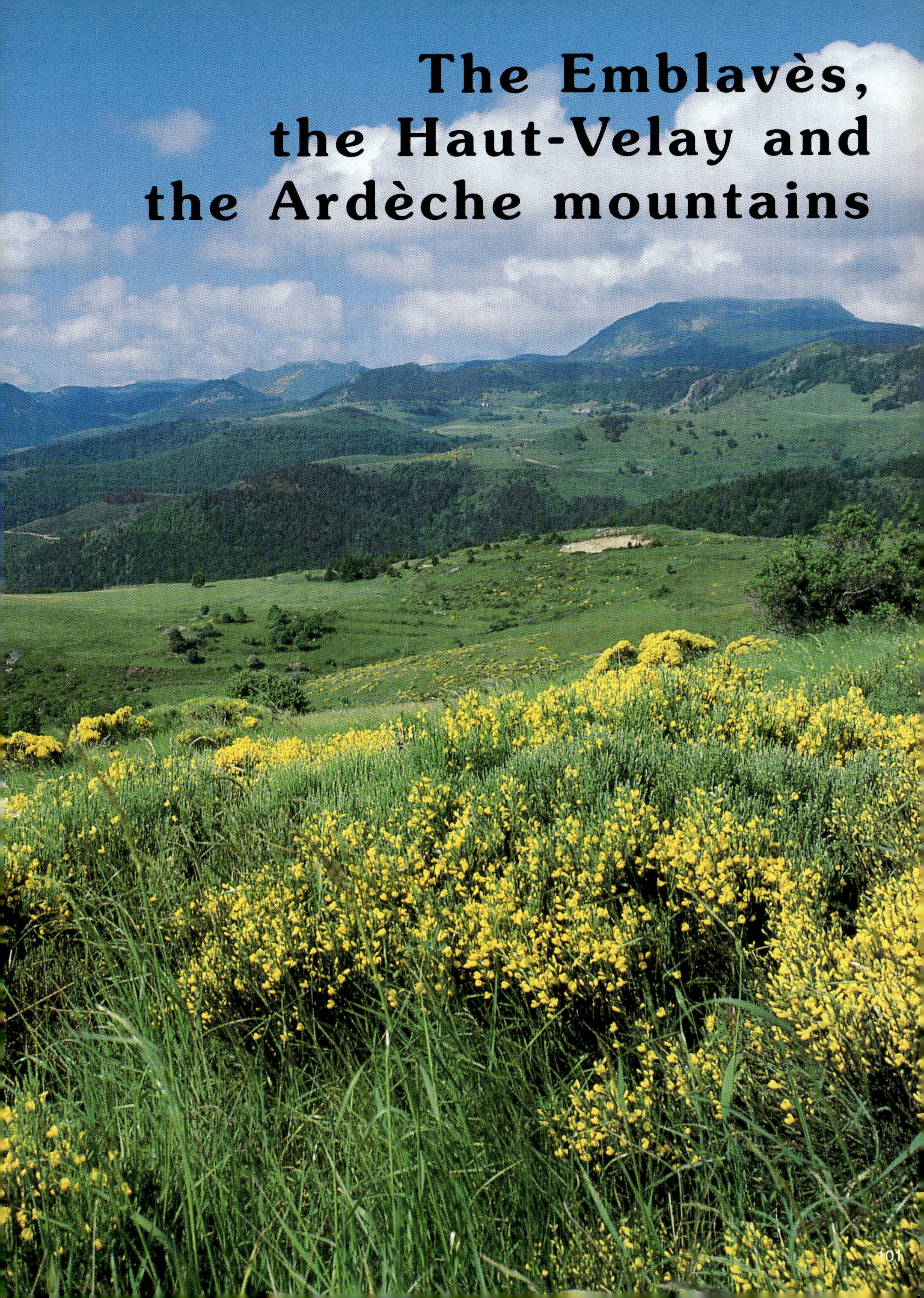

The Emblavès is a small fault trough separated from the Le Puy basin by the granite block of the horst of Chaspinhac. It dates back 13 to 6 million years, but with a series of events very different to that which occurred at Meygal-Mézenc. This form of volcanism also differs from that of Le Puy in that water was not abundant.
The volcanoes of the Emblavès form a profusion of basalt necks and extrusions of phonolite, which are reminiscent of the neighbouring Sucs of the eastern Velay. These landforms are domes, such as the Mont Chéron and the Suc d'Eyme, to the west of Yssingeaux, or tubular, prismatic masses, such as the Mont Plaux, near Saint-Julien-Chapteuil. There are also several tabular volcanic flows, such as the Huche Plate, but they are less common than in the Le Puy basin. The highest points of this area include the Mont Loségal (1,136 m) and the Suc de Jorance (1,182 m).

Above - *The village of Queyrières* and inset, *the columns of the same name.*
Opposite centre - *A typical landscape near Yssingeaux, looking westwards to Saint-Julien-Chapteuil.*
Inset - *The Suc d'Achon.* Bottom - *The suc de Monac.*

Formation of necks

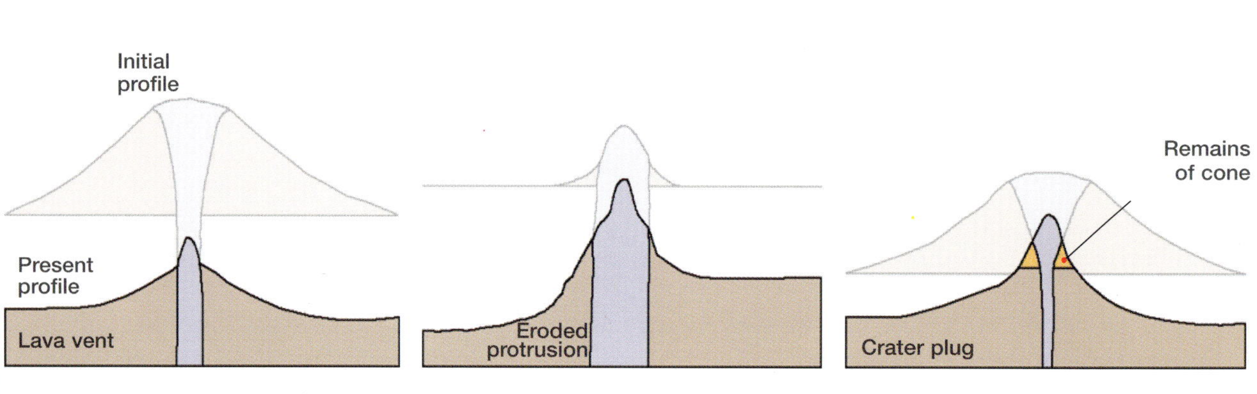

Above - *The Pic du Lisieux with its sought after stone.*
Inset - *The Suc des Ollières, near Yssingeaux.*
Below - *The phonolite quarries in the Emblavès Sucs produce roofing stones of the highest quality.*

The land of phonolite

Following on from the trough of the Emblavès, to the south-east lies the granite horst which supports the Meygal-Mézenc massif. These highlands overlook the collapsed areas of the Boutières in the Ardèche. This geologically highly unusual part of the eastern Velay is known as the "pays des Sucs" and nowhere else in Europe has phonolitic activity occurred to this extent. Nevertheless, if we consider the history of the area as a whole, we note a gradual change in the magma, from the highly fluid initial basalts to the particularly viscous trachytic forms. This chronology may be seen in the remarkable natural cross sections in the Cirque des Boutières, gauged out by erosion in the Ardèche.
11.5 million years ago, activity began in the form of abundant flows of basalt, which continued until 7 million years ago. The accumulation of flows of basalt at first, followed by hawaiites, mugearites

and benmoreites, shows the evolution of the chemistry of the magma towards an increased silica content. This change was confirmed later by the appearance of a multitude of extrusions of phonolite, overlaid with viscous, or almost congealed lavas, which broke through the basalt crust and sometimes culminated directly on the granite of the basement. These eruptions were characterised by the almost total absence of explosive phenomena, which explains the lack of pyroclastic materials in this region, with the exception of the area to the south of the Col du Pertuis, where tuff rich in white granules of phonolite occurs.

To the north, stands the imposing mass of phonolite of the Meygal, which rises to the Grand Testavoyre (1,436 m) the slopes of which are exploited by several roofing stone quarries. Not far away stands the Pic du Lizieux (1,388 m), a dome-flow of the same type as the Meygal.

The Cirque des Boutières, with the Roche des Cuzets.
Inset - *The features on the edge of the cirque, with an accumulation of material ejected by the small strato-volcano in this area.*

Where the Velay and the Haute-Ardèche meet, the grandiose landscape combines the Gerbier de Jonc, on the left, *and the Mézenc, in the background* on the right, *with between them, a host of Sucs, from which stand out the Rocher des Pradoux* in the centre *and the Suc de Sara,* to its right. Inset, on the left*, the Mézenc above Estables,* on the right *at the top the Gerbier de Jonc* *and* at the bottom*, the Gouleyou and the Suc de Touron.*

The peaks of the province

To the south, the lower horizon corresponds to planezes armoured by the initial basalts then, on the highest point of the basement rises the Mézenc (1,753 m). This highest point of the Velay and its neighbour Mont d'Alambre (1,691 m) are again lava-domes and, therefore extrusions. The Signon de Chaudeyrolles (1,454 m) and the Tortue, near Boussoulet, also belong to this group.
The thimble shape that may be seen from Mézenc is evidence of protrusions. Among them, the Gerbier de Jonc (1,551 m) is neither the highest nor most imposing, but its perfect shape, the build

Above - *The "rivers of stone" on the Ardèche slope of the Mézenc.*
Below - *At the summit of the Mézenc, weathered rocks such as those from which roofing stones are taken.*

up of rocks and its location at the source of the Loire, make it one of the most visited in the region. Several sources, including the "true" source emerge at the base of this Suc, where the permeable phonolite and the impermeable basalt flows of the Miocene epoch meet. Other crags are scattered over this plateau not far from the immense drop of the Ardèche slope and, in particular the Coux, together with the Sucs de Montfol, Sépous, Lauzière and Taupernas.

Above - *The Salins falls, with the Mézenc in the background.*
Opposite - *The Roche Pointue.*
Below left - *A volcanic wayside cross at Faye-sur-Lignon.*
Below right - *The Gerbier de Jonc.*

The last eruptions in the eastern Velay

At the foot of the Mézenc opens out the impressive Cirque des Boutières, one of the most remarkable sites in the Massif Central. This area was formed by a small strato-volcano and one of its explosion craters. Carved out by the glaciers of the Quaternary period and by the torrential erosion of the Mediterranean façade, the cirque cuts through ancient flows, whilst later eruptive formations have resisted, making its relief particularly rugged. The area includes Sucs such as the Suc de Touron (1,290 m), which is particularly pointed, or the Roche de Borée, accumulations of scoria, together with remarkable annular intrusions.

These are evidence of late, highly alkaline eruptions (6.3 million years), which passed directly through the granite. This mainly concerns the Rocher des Pradoux and the edifice to which the Suc de Sara (1,520 m), the Suc de la Veine (1,233 m) and dike at Prévenchères belong. They are made up of hypovolcanic rocks which cooled very slowly.

A maar, the Lake of Issarlès. Inset - *The crater of the Cherchemuse.*
Below left - *Saint-Martial, which lies under the Cirque des Boutières.*
Below right - The Gardy farm, under the Roches Borée.
Inset - *The Suc de Sara.*

The end of volcanic activity in the eastern Velay was explosive, as shown by the craters of the maars of the Saint-Front and Issarlès lakes. The latter, appeared less than a million years ago with the neighbouring volcano of Cherchemuse, and covers 90 hectares with a depth of 138 metres, which makes it the largest of its type in the Massif Central. Other maars, the craters of which are now filled, formed as at Chaudeyrolles.

Above - *The maar of Chaudeyrolles with the Mézenc in the background.*
Below - *The Lake of Saint-Front, near Faye-sur-Lignon.*

The Coupe de Jaujac volcano on the southern edge of the Lignon valley.

The Ardèche Cévenne and the Coiron

The Ardèche Cévenne, which is an extension of the eastern Velay and the Montagne, is a volcanic area of great interest rivalling the Chaîne des Puys in the youth of its features.
Volcanic activity in the Ardèche Cévenne followed fractures running north-west - south-east. Up-river from Vals-les-Bains and towards the Gerbier de Jonc, the oldest of these alignments, which is about 80,000 years old, is famous for the Ray-Pic falls where the Bourges and a small tributary pass over the lip of a superb prismatic flow basalt, side by side. This flow, the longest in France, first extends in fragments, then continuously, from Burzet to the course of the Ardèche, in a succession of "giant's causeways" and superb pools surrounded by basalt columns. These features, which remain despite vigorous erosion, are clear evidence of the youth of this eruption. The alignment is also marked by the old maar of the Pic de l'Etoile and the Coupe d'Aizac, a breached cinder cone, at the base of which the Fuels stream cascades after rain, from the top of the Rocher du Fromage, a magnificent prismatic flow.

Above - *The crater of the Coupe d'Aizac, near Vals-les-Bains.*
Below - *The Gravenne de Montpezat, between the Ardèche and the Fontaulière.*

The Ray-Pic falls and a fine accumulation of prismatic basalt.
Inset - *The Suc de Bauzon, (1,471 metres).*

Above - *The Vestide du Pal, the biggest maar in Europe.*

Below - *The Gravenne de Thueyts, disembowelled by a quarry.*

The biggest maar in Europe

Further south, another fracture produced a series of spectacular volcanic manifestations 30,000 years ago, in less than a hundred years. Near Rieutord, the most important feature is the Vestide du Pal, a maar 1.5 km in diameter, dimensions unparalleled in Europe. In its centre, rise four small Strombolian cones, evidence of a later resumption in activity. The debris of the crystalline basement carried off by the cataclysmic explosion of this maar is visible on the Suc du Pal which overlooks the cirque from a height of 1,402 m.
The rest of the fracture is marked by the Gravenne de Montpezat (846 m), a volcano with a breached crater, a flow from which is superimposed on that of the Ray-Pic in the valley of the Fontaulière. We then come to the Gravenne de Thueyts, a cinder cone in which the quarry has revealed large numbers of "cow dung" volcanic bombs. Finally, the Coupe de Jaujac, which also has a breached crater, produced a flow of "blue basalt" in the Lignon valley, where erosion has exposed columns and "giant's causeways".

The Coiron, a balcony overlooking the Rhône

The Coiron is a plateau with scalloped edges which extends some twenty kilometres to the south of Privas, between the edge of the Cévennes and the Rhone valley. The lavas, all basalts, which formed it, came from a major north-west to south-east fault, which is an extension of those of the eastern Velay. The alignment of eruptive outcrops and dikes between the Mézenc and the Crête de Blandine, where the Coiron rises to its highest point of 1,017 metres, is striking.
The Coiron resembles the Aubrac, its contemporary, with an initial period of activity in the late Miocene epoch: this disseminated form of volcanism became increasingly explosive. Later, rises of fluid magma constructed the table formations of the present Coiron, over scoria and tuff. The later tectonic upheaval of the Ardèche Cévenne caused significant inversion in the relief of almost five hundred metres near the Rhône. These lava flows are remarkable at Mirabel, with its fine cliffs. Even more spectacular are the Roche-Chérie, a high neck, the Balmes de Montbrun, caves excavated by man in reddish scoria, and the village of Sceautres, nestling against a volcanic plug.

Above - *The Crête de Blandine, the highest point of the Coiron.*
Below top - *Mirabel and its basalt cliffs.*
Bottom left - *Behind Saint-Pons, the cliffs of the Regard plain.* Right - *Saint-Pons and its plateau.*

At Cap-d'Agde, the rocks and volcanic sand of the Grande Conque.
Inset - *The island of Fort-Brescou, a small submarine volcano.*

The volcanism of the Causses, the Escandorgue and the Bas-Languedoc

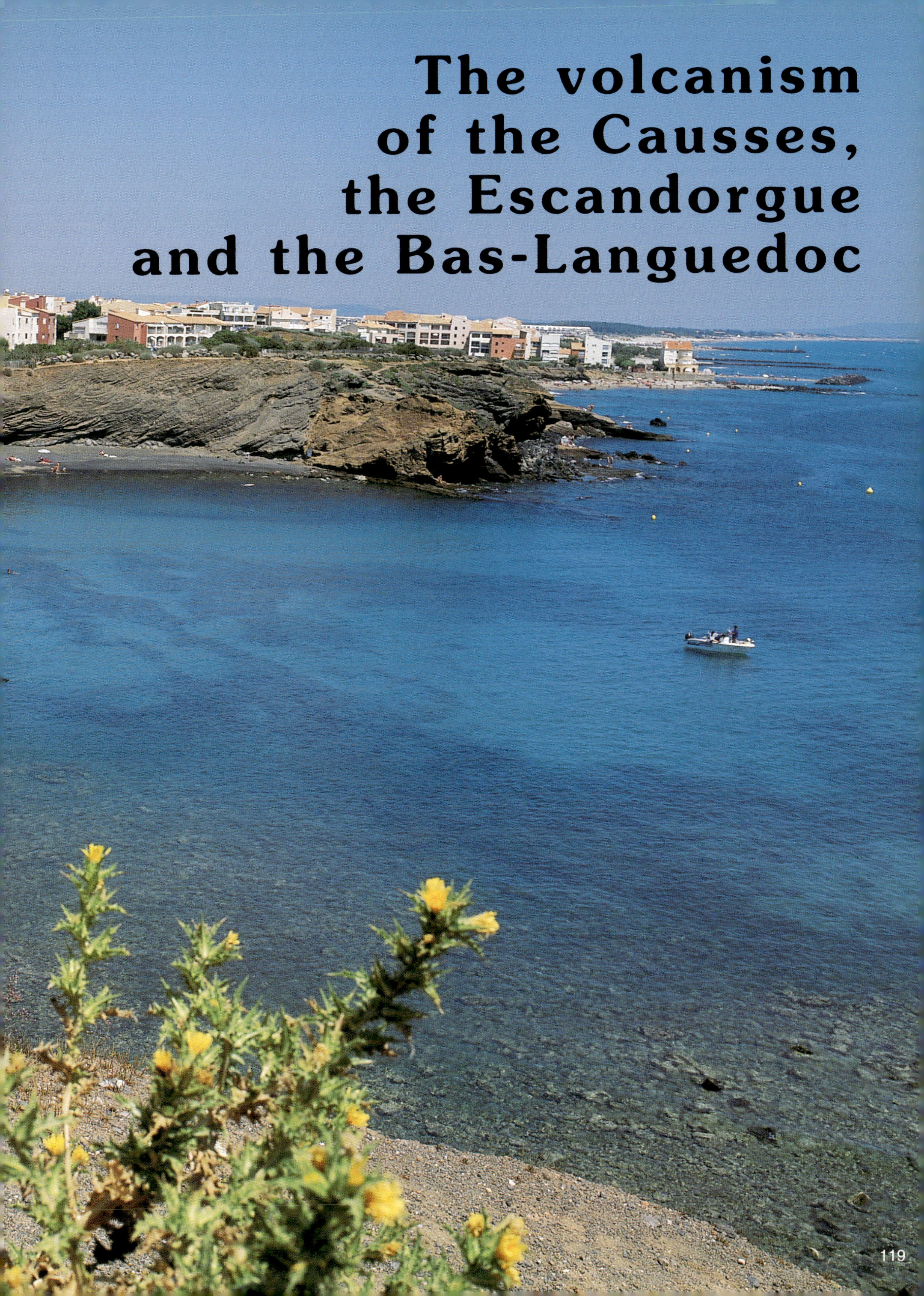

In ancient times, volcanic activity made an intrusion into the limestone kingdom of the Causses. To the south of the great edifices of the Auvergne, lie the first signs of a "southern volcanic train" which runs down to the sea. From the Lot to the Mediterranean, there are more than two hundred occurrences of alkali basalts as this volcanism cut through the sedimentary blocks.

The aborted volcanoes of the Causses

The Jurassic limestones of the Causses blocked the rise of magma so well that the volcanism of this region consists of veins, sills, necks and breccia diatremes filled with clearing debris rather than lavas.
Such formations may be seen near La Canourgue, and thanks to the natural cross section provided by the Tarn gorges. This is the case above Vignes,

Below top - *Sauveterre, on the causse of the same name, which occupies a volcanic butte.*
Bottom left - *Opposite Roquefort, a dark volcanic flow in the middle of the Larzac limestone.*
Right - *Nears Vignes, in the Tarn gorges, a bright white vein of calcite, between layers of basalt.*

Near Le Rozier, the edge of the Méjean causse towers over the Eglazine volcano.
Inset - *In the same area, on the Causse de Sauveterre, a vein of basalt in fissures in the limestone.*

where the river has exposed the basalts of a submarine flow of the Jurassic period, set in the limestone of the slopes of the Méjean and Sauveterre causses. Three kilometres up-river of Le Rozier, a patch of dark rocks is evidence of a volcanic event at the start of the Quaternary period. The accumulation of basalt of the pseudo-volcano of Eglazines, some 9 million years old and which is the vent of an aborted eruption, also dates back to this period.

The thick prismatic flow of the Azinières volcano, on the Causse Rouge, near Millau.

Above - Lake of Le Salagou and the volcanic plateau of Auvernhe on its northern shores.
Below - The front of a flow at Romiguières, to the north of Lodève.

Lava flows of this type have filled certain karstic systems, particularly in the Lodévois. This region, which is mainly formed by a clay depression, experienced discrete effusive activity, in the form of veins and vents. Cleared by erosion, this volcanism now takes the form of irregular crags and tabular features, as on the plateau d'Auvernhe, near Lake of Le Salagou.

The volcanisme of the Sillon Houiller

The Sillon Houiller is an important geological accident which runs between the Auvergne and the Limousin. Volcanic activity occurred in several of the basins along this fault in ancient times: there were rises of rhyolites at Champagnac in the Cantal, tuff ejecta near Messeix, trachytes and rhyolites at Saint-Eloy-les-Mines and Pontaumur and to the south, in the Decazeville basin, andesitic lavas, particularly in the cliffs at Port d'Agrès (Aveyron), 150 metres above the Lot.
Volcanic activity affected other isolated coal basins, such as those at Brassac-les-Mines and Langeac where tuffs and rhyolites may be seen. Finally, at Commentry, coal seams were transformed into coke by the heat of the intrusive rocks.

The dike of La Roque on the shores of Lake of Le Salagou.
Inset - *The basalt columns of Mont Redon.*

Strombolian edifices battered by the waves

To the west of Lodève, the massif of the Escandorgue shows a north-south line of overlapping basalt which runs on to the Larzac and the "Avant-causses". Also seen are Strombolian cones, such as that at Romiguières, and exit points such as the Signal de Bouviala.

In the Bas-Languedoc, the lack of sedimentary cover allowed explosive activity to occur, for example the isolated Strombolian edifices such as the Monts Ramus and the volcano of Roque-Haute at Portiragnes. But we look particularly at the region of Agde, christened the "black city" by Marco Polo, who was astonished to discover its houses built of basalt.

These flows are spectacular at Cap-d'Agde where the cone of a 740,000 year old volcano has been swept away by the sea and where the waves break over its dike. This submarine volcanism extends under the sea, as the island of basalt on which the Fort Brescou is built proves. To the north of Montpellier, opposite several basalt outcrops, another volcanic "island" rises above this shoreline, to the east near Palavas, and on which the famous cathedral of Maguelonne is built.

Finally, further out to sea, some thirty kilometres from the coast, soundings have identified a submarine volcano, which may be evidence of the most recent French eruption...

Left - *The cathedral at Agde, built from dark lava, like Clermont-Ferrand cathedral.*
Below - *The Plagette at Cap-d'Agde and the remains of a volcano washed away by the sea.*
Inset - *Tuffs eroded by the wind and the waves.*

The cathedral of Maguelonne, on a volcanic island now attached to the shore.
Above - *At Cap-d'Agde, a broken lava flow, the blocks of which have been rounded by the waves.*
Top - *Basalt at the extreme tip of Cap-d'Agde.*

Glossary

andesite: *a volcanic rock fairly poor in silica*
aragonite: *a crystalline variety of calcium carbonate*
ash: *lava ejecta of less than 2 mm in size*
basalt: *dark, basic, very fluid lava, which is very common on Earth*
basanite: *a variety of basalt*
Bedded: *said of tuffs piled up in diatremes*
benmoreite: *a variety of basalt*
bomb (spindle, cauliflower or cow dung shaped): *blocks of lava of a few centimetres to two or three metres in size, thrown into the air where they take on specific forms*
breccia: *rock made up of broken fragments gathered together in a cement of fine particles*
calcite: *crystallised calcium carbonate*
caldera: *circular collapse caused by the emptying of a magma chamber*
cheire: *an Auvergne name for lava flows with a scoriaceous, chaotic surface*
cinerite: *consolidated volcanic ash*
conglomerate: *detrital rock formed of fragments torn away from pre-existing rock and agglomerated by a cement*
couze: *the name of the streams in the eastern part of the Cézalier and the Monts Dore*
crystal form: *the appearance of a rock that depends on the conditions under which it was formed*
crystalline (basement): *all granites that form the continental basement*
crust: *the superficial part of the Earth*
cumulo-dome: *a volcano formed by a dome of viscous lava that accumulated around its exit point*
base surge: *a ring-shaped nuée ardente which forms in the mouth of a crater and at the base of a vertical explosive column, typical of the phreatomagmatic explosions*
Columns (volcanic): *the prismatic formation of parallel polygonal columns, several metres high, in a lava flow, at the end of the cooling process*
diapir: *a mass of materials the heat and therefore lower density of which causes to rise through the upper layer of the Earth's crust, like a bubble, and which gradually goes from the solid state to the liquid state until it forms a magma chamber*
diatomite: *a siliceous sedimentary rock of biological origin (generally formed by minuscule skeletons of plankton)*
diatreme: *a volcanic vent filled with breccia or bedded tuff*
dike: *a vein of lava exposed by erosion, which takes the form of a wall*
doreite: *a dark trachyandesite typical of the Monts Dore*
effusive (activity): *refers to an eruption that produces lava flows*
erratic (block): *refers to blocks transported great distances from their point of origin by ancient glaciers*
extrusion: *an outpouring of pasty volcanic rock which may form a needle or dome*
facies: *the appearance of a rock that depends on the conditions under which it was formed*
fumerolic: *related to the fairly regular, non-explosive emanations of gas which often precede or follow eruptions*
gabbro: *a coarse-grained eruptive rock containing pyroxene*
geothermal gradient: *variation in the temperature of the Earth according to depth*
hawaiite: *a variety of basalt*
Hercynian: *concerns the geology of the Palaeozoic era*
horn: *pyramidal feature formed by the action of glaciers*
horst: *a block of land raised up between faults*
hyaloclastite: *breccia or tuff produced by the fragmentation of lava due to sudden contact with water*
ignimbrite: *a deposit of welded pyroclastic flows of small fragments*
inversion (of relief): *revealing up of land (for example, lava flows) which is more resistant to erosion than the land in which in which it was originally found*
karstic: *refers to a specific form of erosion in limestone plateaux*
Katmaian: *related to the eruption of Mount*

126

Katmai in Alaska in June 1912, which led to a better understanding of pyroclastic mechanisms
lahar: *a massive mudflow caused by the torrential rain provoked by pyroclastic eruptions*
lapilli: *volcanic rock fragmented by eruptions of between 2 mm and a few centimetres*
maar: *a large explosion crater that cuts out the surrounding land like a pastry cutter*
magma: *a pasty material at high temperature (at least 600°C) which forms in the outer layers of the Earth*
mantle: *a layer of magma 2,900 km thick under the crust and around the core*
marl: *clayey limestone*
metamorphism: *the transformation of rock under the effects of temperature and pressure*
Miocene: *an epoch of the Tertiary period from 25 to 9 million years ago*
morainic: *said of rock debris transported by glaciers*
mugearite: *a variety of trachyandesite*
neck: *the old vent of a volcano filled with lava and exposed by erosion*
nuée ardente: *a pyroclastic flow of gases and burning ash, which may be of various kinds (Pelean, fallback, katmaian, etc.)*
ordanchite: *lava similar to basalt*
palagonite: *a yellow hydrated glass which appears when molten basalt comes into contact with water*
Pelean: *a type of eruption that refers to those of Mount Pelée in Martinique, in 1902-1905 and 1929-1932*
peperite: *a pyroclastic rock specific to the Limagne, made up of granules of basalt in a marl-limestone cement*
phonolite: *a variety of dark, greenish trachyte, that splits into slabs that ring when struck*
phreatomagmatism: *all eruptive manifestations caused by rising magma coming into contact with unconfined groundwater or water on the surface*
planeze: *a slightly inclined, triangular plateau of basaltic lava on the flank of a strato-volcano*
Plinian (eruption): *a cataclysmic eruption of the type of that of Vesuvius in AD 79 and which killed the naturalist Pliny the Elder*
plug: *lava that has solidified in the bottom of the crater of a volcano*
pozzolana: *a term with no geological significance used in the Auvergne to describe materials quarried from the cinder cones of the Chaîne des Puys and the Devès*
protrusion: *a volcanic edifice formed by the vertical rise of a piston of semi-rigid lava*
pumice: *a very porous, glassy pyroclastic rock*
pyroclastic rocks: *incoherent rocks fragmented by the expansion of gas during eruptions*
pyroxene: *a mineral present in volcanic rocks*
rhyolite: *a lava rich in silica*
rift: *a tectonic trough, several hundreds or thousands of kilometres long, that corresponds to a fracture zone in the Earth's crust*
sancyite: *a variety of trachyte*
scoria: *fragments of frothy lava ejected in liquid form by the crater where they form fairly viscous lava flows on the surface*
silica: *a very hard, solid body which forms more than half of the Earth's crust*
sill: *a vein lying parallel to the layers of the host ground*
strato-volcano: *a compound volcanic edifice formed over a long period with a complex shape*
Strombolian: *refers to the type of eruption seen on Stromboli in Italy, characterised by moderate explosiveness and the regular ejection of scoria*
Surtseyen: *a type of eruption where fluid magma encounters a wide, shallow expanse of water*
tectonic: *all deformations and fractures affecting geological ground during and after their formation*
trachyte: *a volcanic rock rich in silica*
tuff: *a friable pyroclastic rock*
vein: *a body of rock which cuts through the surrounding ground by filling a fissure (see dike)*

A block of pozzolane.

Unboundcover
The craters of the Puys de Jume and de la Coquille (Puy-de-Dôme).

Versions françaises dépôt légal juillet 2002
ISBN 978-2-913381-03-2 version brochée française réimprimée en mars 2010
ISBN 978-2-913381-04-9 version reliée française réimprimée en avril 2004

Versions étrangères dépot légal juillet 2002
ISBN 978-2-913381-12-4 version en allemand « Berühmte & weniger bekannte Vulkane im Zentralmassiv » réimprimée en mars 2010
ISBN 978-2-913381-13-1 version en anglais « Known & little-known volcanoes of the Massif central » réimprimée en mars 2010

Imprimerie Clerc - Saint-Amand-Montrond - Cher (France)

Rue Becquerel - Z.A. de l'Artière - 63110 Beaumont
Téléphone 33 (0)4 73 27 43 00 - Fax 33 (0)4 73 26 26 12
www.editions-debaisieux.fr